Tomorrow, and tomorrow, and tomorrow
Creeps in this petty pace from day to day,
To the last syllable of recorded time;
And all our yesterdays have lighted fools
The way to dusty death. Out, out, brief candle!
Life's but a walking shadow, a poor player
That struts and frets his hour upon the stage
And then is heard no more. It is a tale
Told by an idiot, full of sound and fury,
Signifying nothing.

THE TRAGEDY OF MACBETH
Act V, Scene 5

THE TRAGEDY OF MACBETH

William Shakespeare

with Connections

HOLT, RINEHART AND WINSTON
Harcourt Brace & Company

Austin • New York • Orlando • Atlanta • San Francisco
Boston • Dallas • Toronto • London

There are good reasons for believing that *Macbeth* was written in 1605–1606 and performed at Hampton Court in 1606 before King James I of England and his brother-in-law, Christian of Denmark. The play seems to have been written to please James and thereby to further the fortunes of Shakespeare's theatrical company, the King's Men. James was a writer and two of his favorite subjects were his ancestry and witchcraft, both of which are prominent in the play. Further evidence that Shakespeare was hoping to please James can be found in the flattering portrait of Banquo, from whom the Stuarts claimed to be descended. James was the ninth Stuart monarch.

Cover illustration of the witches of *Macbeth* based on a woodcut by Henry Fuseli, courtesy Corbis-Bettmann.

This edition of *The Tragedy of Macbeth* is published by Holt, Rinehart and Winston as part of the HRW Classics Library.

For permission to reprint copyrighted material, grateful acknowledgment is made to the following sources:

Dutton Signet, a division of Penguin Books USA Inc.: From the annotations from *Macbeth* by William Shakespeare. Copyright © 1963 and renewed © 1991 by Sylvan Barnet for introduction and annotations.
Farrar, Straus & Giroux, Inc.: Canto XXXIV from *The Inferno of Dante: A New Verse Translation* by Robert Pinsky. Copyright © 1994 by Farrar, Straus & Giroux, Inc. Translation copyright © 1994 by Robert Pinsky.
John Hawkins & Associates, Inc.: "Macbeth and the Witches" from *Twisted Tales from Shakespeare* by Richard Armour. Copyright © 1957 by Richard Armour.

Printed in the United States of America
ISBN 0-03-052233-1   2 3 4 5 6 043 99 98

CONTENTS

The Renaissance Theater

Drama as Teacher: The Forerunners

Even before the Renaissance, the English had been writing and performing plays for several centuries. Some scholars believe that medieval drama evolved from church ceremonies such as the dialogue songs performed at Easter Eve services. In these tiny playlets three women would appear at a door representing the tomb of Christ and guarded by an angel. The angel would ask in Latin, "Whom do you seek?" and then he would announce the Resurrection.

From this obscure beginning, drama moved out of the churches and into the marketplaces of towns. There, in the 1300s and 1400s, various workers' guilds cooperated in staging cycles of plays that dramatized the whole history of the human race as then understood: its creation by God, its fall through the wiles of Satan, its life in Old Testament times, its redemption by Christ, and its final judgment at the end of the world. Parts of four cycles of these plays have been preserved, and they are named after the towns where they probably originated: York, Chester, Coventry, and Wakefield. Gradually the plays became less religious, often relying on *deus ex machina* (an artificial device arbitrarily used to resolve a plot), and comedy was incorporated into them. The wife of Noah, for instance, makes a great fuss about entering the ark and is carried kicking and screaming aboard. Comic scenes like this one provide an early example of English skill in mixing the comic with the serious in drama. The most notable play of the period just before the Renaissance is *Everyman,* based on a Dutch original.

Several kinds of plays, then, were written and produced before the Renaissance: **miracle** and **mystery plays,** which taught people stories from the Bible and saints' legends; **moralities,** which taught people how to live and die; and, starting in the early 1500s, a new kind of play called an **interlude.** Interludes were one-act plays, some of them indistinguishable from moralities, others rowdy and farcical. With the interludes the playwrights stopped being anonymous. Even before the new humanist learning came in, there were strong dramatic traditions that the great Renaissance playwrights knew about.

Old Traditions, New Theaters

By the mid–sixteenth century, the art of drama in England was three centuries old, but the idea of housing it in a permanent building was new. Even after theaters were built, plays were still regularly performed in improvised spaces when acting companies toured the provinces or presented their plays in the large houses of royalty and nobility.

In 1576, James Burbage, the father of Shakespeare's partner and fellow actor Richard Burbage, built the first public theater and called it, appropriately, the Theater. Shortly thereafter a second playhouse, called the Curtain, was erected. Both of these were in a northern suburb of London, where they would not offend the staid residents of London proper. Then came the Rose, the Swan, the Fortune, the Globe, the Red Bull, and the Hope—far more public theaters than in any other European capital.

The Globe: "This Wooden O"

The Globe is the most famous of the public theaters because the company that Shakespeare belonged to owned it. Many of his plays received their first performances there. It was built out of timbers salvaged from the Theater, which was demolished in 1599. Unfortunately, the plans for the Globe have not survived, though there still exist old panoramic drawings of London in which its exterior is pictured. But the most important sources of information about the theater's structure are the plays themselves, with their stage directions and other clues.

Most scholars now accept as accurate the reconstruction of the Globe published by C. Walter Hodges. The theater had three main parts: the building proper, the stage, and the tiring house, or backstage area, with the flag flying from its peak to indicate that there would be a performance that day.

A wooden structure three stories high, the building proper surrounded a spacious inner yard open to the sky. It was probably a sixteen-sided polygon. Any structure with that many sides would appear circular, so it is not surprising that Shakespeare referred to the Globe as "this wooden O" in his play *Henry V.* There were probably only two entrances to the building, one for the public and one for the theater company. But there may have been another public door used as an exit, because when the Globe burned down in 1613, the crowd escaped quickly and safely.

General admission to the theater cost one penny; this entitled a spectator to be a groundling, which meant he or she could stand in the yard. Patrons paid a little more to mount up into the galleries, where there were seats and a better view of the stage. The most expensive seats were chairs set right on the stage along its two sides. People who wanted to be conspicuous rented them, though they must have been a great nuisance to the rest of the audience and the actors. A public theater held a surprisingly large number of spectators—three thousand, according to two contemporary accounts. Since the spectators must have been squeezed together, it is no wonder that the authorities always closed the theaters during plague epidemics.

Up Close and Personal

The stage jutted halfway out into the yard, so that the actors were in much closer contact with the audience than actors are in modern theaters. Thus, every tiny nuance of an actor's perform-ance could affect the audience. The actors were highly trained, and they could sing, dance, declaim, wrestle, fence, clown, roar, weep, and whisper. Large, sensational effects were also plentiful. Spectators loved to see witches or devils emerge through the trapdoor in the stage, which everybody pretended led down to hell, just as everybody pretended that the ceiling over part of the stage was the heavens. This ceiling was painted with elaborate suns, moons, and stars, and it contained a trapdoor through which angels, gods, and spirits could be lowered on a wire and even flown over the other actors' heads.

Behind the Scenes

The third part of the theater was the tiring (from *tire,* an archaic form of *attire*) house, a tall building that contained machinery and dressing rooms and that provided a two-story back wall for the stage. Hodges's drawing of the Globe shows that this wall contained a gallery above and a curtained space below. The gallery had multiple purposes, depending on what play was being performed: Spectators could sit there, musicians could perform there, or parts of the play could be acted there—as if on balconies, towers, hills, and the like. The curtained area below the gallery was used mainly for "discoveries" of things prepared in advance and hidden from the audience until the proper time. In Shakespeare's *Merchant of Venice,* for example, the curtain is drawn to reveal three small chests, one of which hides the hero-ine's picture. Apparently this curtained area was too small, too shallow, and too far out of the sight of some spectators to be used as a performance space. If a performer were "discovered" behind the curtains (as Marlowe's Dr. Faustus is discovered in his study), he would quickly move out onto the stage to be seen and heard better. When large properties such as thrones, beds, desks, and so on were pushed through the curtains onto the stage, the audience would know at once that the action was taking place indoors. When the action shifted to the outdoors, the property could be pulled back behind the curtain.

The Power of Make-Believe

Renaissance audiences took for granted that the theater cannot show "reality": Whatever happens on the stage is make-believe. When the people in the audience saw actors carrying lanterns, they knew it was night, even though the sun was shining brightly overhead. Often, instead of seeing a scene, they heard it described, as when Shakespeare has a character exclaim over a sunrise,

> But look, the morn in russet mantle clad
> Walks o'er the dew of yon high eastward hill.
> —*Hamlet,* Act I, Scene 1, lines 166–167

When a forest setting was called for, there was no painted scenery imitating real trees, bushes, flowers, and so on. Instead, a few bushes and small trees might be pushed onto the stage, and then the actors spoke lines that evoked images in the spectators' minds. In *As You Like It,* Rosalind simply looks around and announces, "Well, this is the forest of Arden." As the theatrical historian Gerald Bentley put it, Renaissance drama was "a drama of persons, not a drama of places."

Pomp and Pageantry

The scenery may have been kept to a minimum, but the theaters themselves were ornate. The interiors were painted brightly, with many decorations, and the space at the rear of the stage could be covered with colorful tapestries or hangings. Costumes were rich, elaborate, and expensive. The manager-producer Philip Henslowe once paid twenty pounds (then an enormous sum) for a single cloak for one of his actors to wear. Henslowe's lists of theatrical properties mention chariots, fountains, dragons, beds, tents, thrones, booths, and wayside crosses, among other things.

The audience also enjoyed the processions—religious, royal, military—that occurred in many plays. These would enter the stage from one door, cross the stage, and then exit by the other door. A few quick costume changes as the actors passed through the tiring house could double and triple the apparent number of people in a procession.

Music Most Eloquent

When people went to the London theater, they expected not only to see a tragedy or comedy acted but also to hear music, both vocal and instrumental. Trumpets announced the beginning of the play and important arrivals and departures within the play. High up in the gallery, musicians played between acts and at other appropriate times during the performance. And scattered throughout most of the plays, especially the comedies, were songs.

The songs in Shakespeare's plays are the best of this kind that have come down to us, for Shakespeare excelled in lyric and in dramatic poetry. He included a great variety of songs in his plays: sad, happy, comic, thoughtful songs, each one adapted to the play and scene in which it occurs and to the character who performs it. Some of the songs advance the dramatic action, some help establish the mood of a scene, and some reveal character. Like this invitation to love (from the comedy *Twelfth Night*), all of these songs are fresh and spontaneous, not contrived and artificial.

> O mistress mine, where are you roaming?
> O, stay and hear, your true love's coming,
>   That can sing both high and low.

Trip no further, pretty sweeting;
Journeys end in lovers meeting,
   Every wise man's son doth know . . .

What is love? 'tis not hereafter;
Present mirth hath present laughter;
   What's to come is still unsure.
In delay there lies no plenty;
Then come kiss me, sweet and twenty;
   Youth's a stuff will not endure.

Unfortunately, most of the original music for Shakespeare's songs has been lost. But just as the plays themselves have inspired many composers of music for opera, orchestra, and ballet, so have the songs from the plays been set to music right up to the present.

Varying the Venue

The acting companies performed in two other kinds of spaces: in the great halls of castles and manor houses and in indoor, fully covered theaters in London.

For performances in a great hall, a theater company must have had a portable booth stage. In these buildings the usual entertainment was bearbaiting, a sport in which a bear is attacked by dogs. The bear pits were vile places, but their temporary stages could easily accommodate any play except for ones requiring the use of heavens overhanging the stage.

Something like this booth stage may also have been used in private theaters like the Blackfriars, which Shakespeare's company, the King's Men, acquired in 1608. One great advantage of the Blackfriars—a disused monastery that was entirely roofed over—was that the company could perform there in cold weather and, since artificial lighting always had to be used, at night. Thus, the King's Men could put on plays throughout the year, increasing profits for the shareholders, among them Shakespeare.

William Shakespeare
(1564–1616)

Every literate person has heard of Shakespeare, the author of more than 36 remarkable plays and more than 150 poems. Over the centuries these literary works have made such a deep impression on the human race that all sorts of fancies, legends, and theories have been invented about their author. There are even those who say that somebody other than Shakespeare wrote the works that bear his name, although these people cannot agree on who, among a dozen candidates, this other author actually was. Such speculation is based on the misconception that little is known about Shakespeare's life; in fact, Shakespeare's life is better documented than the life of any other dramatist of the time except perhaps for Ben Jonson, a writer who seems almost modern in the way he publicized himself. Jonson was an honest, blunt, and outspoken man who knew Shakespeare well; for a time the two dramatists wrote for the same theatrical company, and Shakespeare even acted in Jonson's plays. Often ungenerous in his judgments of other writers, Jonson published a poem praising Shakespeare, asserting that he was superior to all Greek, Roman, and other English dramatists, predicting that he would be "not of an age, but for all time." Jonson's judgment is now commonly accepted, and his prophecy has come true.

The Years in Stratford-on-Avon

Shakespeare was born in Stratford-on-Avon, a historic and prosperous market town in Warwickshire, and was christened in the parish church there on April 26, 1564. His father was John

Shakespeare, a merchant once active in the town government; his mother—born Mary Arden—came from a prominent family in the county. Presumably, for seven years or so, William attended the Stratford grammar school, where he obtained an excellent education in Latin, the Bible, and English composition. (The students had to translate Latin works into English and then turn them back into Latin.) After leaving school, he may have been apprenticed to a butcher, but because he shows in his plays very detailed knowledge of many different crafts and trades, speculators have proposed a number of different occupations that he could have had. At eighteen, Shakespeare married Anne Hathaway, the twenty-six-year-old daughter of a farmer living near Stratford. They had three children, a daughter named Susanna and twins named Hamnet and Judith. We don't know how the young Shakespeare supported his family, but according to tradition, he taught school for a few years. The two daughters grew up and married; the son died when he was eleven.

Off to London

To be a dramatist, one had to be in London, where the theater was flourishing in the 1580s. Exactly when Shakespeare left his family and moved to London (there is no evidence that his wife was ever in the city) is uncertain; scholars say that he probably arrived there in 1587. It is certain that he was busy and successful in the London theater by 1592, when a fellow dramatist named Robert Greene attacked him in print and ridiculed a passage in his early play *Henry VI*.

From 1592 on, there is ample documentation of Shakespeare's life and works. We know where he lived in London, at least approximately when his plays were produced and printed, and even how he spent his money. From 1594 until his retirement in about 1613, he was a member of one company, which also included the great tragic actor Richard

Burbage and the popular clown Will Kemp. Although actors and others connected with the theater had very low status legally, in practice they enjoyed the patronage of noblemen and even royalty. It is a mistake to think of Shakespeare as an obscure actor who somehow wrote great plays; he was well-known even as a young man. He first became famous as the author of a bestseller, an erotic narrative poem called *Venus and Adonis* (1593). This poem, as well as the more serious poem *The Rape of Lucrece* (1594), was dedicated to a rich and extravagant young nobleman, the earl of Southampton. The dedication of *Lucrece* suggests that Shakespeare and his wealthy patron were on very friendly terms.

Shakespeare's Early Plays: Variety and Prosperity

Among Shakespeare's earliest plays are the following, with the generally but not universally accepted dates of their first performances: *Richard III* (1592–1593), a chronicle or history play about a deformed usurper who became king of England; *The Comedy of Errors* (1592–1593), a rowdy farce about mistaken identity, based on a Latin play; *Titus Andronicus* (1593–1594), a blood-and-thunder tragedy full of rant and atrocities; *The Taming of the Shrew, The Two Gentlemen of Verona,* and *Love's Labor's Lost* (all 1593–1595), three agreeable comedies; and *Romeo and Juliet* (1594–1595), a poetic tragedy about ill-fated lovers—the Shakespeare play still most frequently taught in schools. The extraordinary thing about these plays is not so much their immense variety—each one is quite different from all the others—but the fact that they are all regularly revived and performed on stages all over the world today.

Years of Prosperity

By 1596, Shakespeare was beginning to prosper. He had his father apply to the Heralds' College for a coat of arms that the family could display, signifying that they were "gentlefolk," or people of high social standing. On Shakespeare's family crest is a falcon shaking a spear. To support this claim to gentility, Shakespeare bought New Place, a handsome house and grounds in Stratford, a place so commodious and elegant that the queen of England once stayed there after Shakespeare's daughter Susanna inherited it. Shakespeare also, in 1599, joined with a few other members of his company, now called the Lord Chamberlain's Men, to finance a new theater—the famous Globe—on the south side of the Thames. The "honey-tongued Shakespeare," as he was called in a book about English literature published in 1598, was now earning money as a playwright, an actor, and a shareholder in a theater. By 1600, Shakespeare was regularly associating with members of the aristocracy, and six of his plays had been given command performances at the court of Queen Elizabeth.

During the last years of Elizabeth I's reign, Shakespeare completed his cycle of plays about England during the Wars of the Roses: *Richard II* (1595–1596), both parts of *Henry IV* (1596–1597), and *Henry V* (1599). Also in this period he wrote the tragedy *Julius Caesar* (1599)—and the comedies that are most frequently performed today: *A Midsummer Night's Dream* (1595–1596), *The Merchant of Venice* (1596–1597), *Much Ado About Nothing* (1598–1599), *As You Like It* (1598–1600), and *Twelfth Night* (1600–1601). And finally, at this time he wrote or rewrote *Hamlet* (1600–1601), the tragedy that, of all his tragedies, has provoked the most varied and controversial interpretations from critics, scholars, and actors. Shakespeare indeed prospered under Queen Elizabeth; according to an old tradition, she asked him to write *The Merry Wives of Windsor* (1600–1601) because she wanted to see the merry, fat old knight Sir John Falstaff (of the Henry plays) in love.

Shakespeare prospered even more under Elizabeth's successor, King James of Scotland. Fortunately for Shakespeare's company, as it turned out, James's royal entry into London in 1603 had to be postponed for several months because the plague was raging in the city. While waiting for the epidemic to subside, the royal court stayed in various palaces outside London. Shakespeare's company took advantage of this situation and, since the city theaters were closed, performed several plays for the court and the new king. Shakespeare's plays delighted James, for he loved literature and was starved for pleasure after the grim experience of ruling Scotland for many years. He immediately took the company under his patronage, renamed them the King's Men, gave them patents to perform anywhere in the realm, provided them with special clothing for state occasions, increased their salaries, and appointed their chief members, including Shakespeare, to be grooms of the royal chamber. All this patronage brought such prosperity to Shakespeare that he was able to make some very profitable real estate investments in Stratford and London.

Shakespeare's "Tragic Period": Beyond Experience

In the early years of the seventeenth century, while his financial affairs were flourishing and everything was apparently going very well for him, Shakespeare wrote his greatest tragedies: *Hamlet* (already mentioned), *Othello* (1601–1602), *King Lear* (1605), *Macbeth* (1605–1606), and *Antony and Cleopatra* (1606–1607). Because these famous plays are so preoccupied with evil, violence, and death, some people feel that Shakespeare must have been unhappy and depressed when he wrote them. Moreover, such people find even the comedies he wrote at this time more sour than sweet: *All's Well That Ends Well* (1602–1603) and *Measure for Measure* (1604). And so, instead of paying tribute to Shakespeare's powerful imagination, which is everywhere evident, these people invent a "tragic period" in Shakespeare's biography, and they search for personal crises in his private life. When they cannot find these agonies, they invent them. To be sure, in 1607, an actor named Edmund Shakespeare, who may well have been William's younger brother, died in London. But by 1607, Shakespeare's alleged "tragic period" was almost over.

It is quite wrong to assume a one-to-one correspondence between writers' lives and their works, because writers must be allowed to imagine whatever they can. It is especially wrong in the case of a writer like Shakespeare, who wrote not to express himself but to satisfy the patrons of the theater that he and his partners owned. Shakespeare must have repeatedly given the audience just what it wanted; otherwise, he could not have made so much money from the theater. To insist that he had to experience and personally feel everything that he wrote about is absurd. He wrote about King Lear, who curses his two monstrous daughters for treating him very badly; in contrast, what evidence there is suggests that Shakespeare got along very well with his own daughters. And so we should think of the years 1600–1607 as glorious rather than tragic, because in them Shakespeare's productivity was at its peak. It seems very doubtful that a depressed person would write plays like these. In fact, they would likely make their creator feel exhilarated rather than sad.

The Last Years: Continued Diversity

In about 1610, Shakespeare decided that, having made a considerable sum from his plays and theatrical enterprises, he would retire to his handsome house in Stratford, a place he had never forgotten, though he seems to have kept his life there rather separate from his life in London. His retirement was not complete, for the records show that after he returned to Stratford he still took part in the management of the King's Men and their two theaters: the Globe, a polygonal building opened in 1599 and used for performances in good weather, and the Blackfriars, acquired in 1608 and used for indoor performances. Shakespeare's works in this period show no signs of diminished creativity, except that in some years he wrote one play instead of the customary two, and they continue to illustrate the great diversity of his genius. Among them are the tragedies *Timon of Athens* (1607–1608) and *Coriolanus* (1607–1608) and five plays that have been variously classified as comedies, romances, or tragi-comedies: *Pericles* (1607–1608), *Cymbeline* (1609–1610), *The Winter's Tale* (1610–1611), *The Tempest* (1611–1612), and *The Two Noble Kinsmen* (1612). His last English-history play, *Henry VIII* (1613), contained a tribute to Queen Elizabeth—a some-what tardy tribute, because, unlike most of the other poets of the day, Shakespeare did not praise her in print when she died in 1603. (Some scholars argue, on very little evidence, that he was an admirer of the earl of Essex, a former intimate of Elizabeth whom she had beheaded for rebellion.) During the first perform-ance of *Henry VIII,* in June of 1613, the firing of the cannon at the end of Act I set the Globe on fire (it had a thatched roof), and it burned to the ground. Only one casualty is recorded: A bottle of ale had to be poured on a man whose breeches were burning. Fortunately, the company had the Blackfriars in which to perform until the Globe was rebuilt and reopened in 1614.

Shakespeare's last recorded visit to London was made with his son-in-law Dr. John Hall in November 1614, though he may have gone down to the city afterward because he con-tinued to own property there, including a building very near the Blackfriars Theater. Probably, though, he spent most of the last two years of his life at New Place, with his daughter Susanna Hall (and his granddaughter Elizabeth) living nearby. He died on April 23, 1616, and was buried under the floor of Stratford Church, with this epitaph warning posterity not to dig him up and transfer him to the graveyard outside the church—a common practice in those days to make room for newer corpses:

> Good friend, for Jesus' sake forbear
> To dig the dust enclosèd here!
> Blest be the man that spares these stones,
> And curst be he that moves my bones.

A Complete Man of the Theater

Shakespeare was a complete man of the theater who created works specifically for his own acting company and his own stage. He had, for instance, to provide good parts in every play for the principal performers in the company, including the comedians acting in tragedies. Since there were no actresses, he had to limit the number of female parts in his plays and create them in such a way that they could readily be taken by boys. For instance, although there are many fathers in the plays, there are very few mothers: While boys could be taught to flirt and play shy, acting maternal would be difficult for them. Several of Shakespeare's young women characters disguise themselves as young men early in Act I—an easy solution to the problem of boys' portraying girls. Shakespeare also had to provide the words for songs because theatergoers expected singing in every play; furthermore, the songs had to be devised so that they would exhibit the talents of particular actors with good voices. Since many of the plays contain many characters, and since there was a limited number of actors in the company, Shakespeare had to arrange for doubling and even tripling of roles: That is, a single actor would have to perform more than one part. Since, of course, an actor could impersonate only one character at a time, Shakespeare had to plan his scenes carefully so that nobody would ever have to be onstage in two different roles at the same time. A careful study of the plays shows that Shakespeare handled very masterfully all these technical problems of dramaturgy.

Never Out of Print

Although the plays are primarily performance scripts, from earliest times the public has wanted to read them as well as to see them staged. In every generation, people have felt that the plays contain so much wisdom, so much knowledge of human nature, so much remarkable poetry that they need to be pondered in private as well as enjoyed in public. Most readers have agreed with what the poet John Dryden said about Shakespeare's "soul": The man who wrote the plays may be elusive, but he was obviously a genius whose lofty imagination is matched by his sympathy for all kinds of human behavior. Reading the plays, then, is a rewarding experience in itself; it is also an excellent preparation for seeing them performed on stage or on film.

Shakespeare's contemporaries were so eager to read his plays that enterprising publishers did everything possible, including stealing them, to make them available. Of course, the company generally tried to keep the plays unpublished because they did not want them performed by rival companies. Even so, eighteen plays were published in small books called quartos before Shakespeare's partners collected and published them after his death. This collection, known as the "first folio" because of its large size, was published in 1623. Surviving copies of this folio are regarded as valuable treasures today. But, of course, the general reader need not consult any of the original texts of Shakespeare, because his works never go out of print; they are always available in many different languages and many different formats. The plays that exist in two different versions (one in a quarto and one in the folio) have provided scholars with endless matter for speculation about what Shakespeare actually intended the text to be. Indeed, every aspect of Shakespeare has been, and continues to be, thoroughly studied and written about by literary and historical scholars, theater and film people, experts in many fields, and amateurs of every stripe. No wonder he is mistakenly regarded as a great mystery.

The Sources of the Play

Shakespeare's play *Macbeth* conforms to the general rule of Renaissance tragedies, in which the drama had to be about real people whose deeds are recorded in history. (Renaissance comedies, on the other hand, concerned the imaginary doings of fictitious characters.) Shakespeare took the main events of Macbeth's career as king of Scotland (1040–1057) from Raphael Holinshed's *Chronicles of England, Scotland, and Ireland* (1577), the book that provided Shakespeare with historical material for many of his plays. But there are striking differences between his account of Macbeth and Holinshed's. The historical Macbeth had a much more legitimate claim to King Duncan's throne than Shakespeare's Macbeth did. The historical Macbeth gained the throne with the help of other nobles dissatisfied with King Duncan, and he ruled rather successfully. In contrast, Shakespeare's Macbeth has no supporters except his wife, whose strong and ambitious nature Shakespeare develops from a brief statement in the history. And in the play, the reign of Macbeth and his wife brings nothing but violence and disaster to Scotland.

One explanation for these changes to Holinshed's story is that Shakespeare wanted to explore—from a safe distance—the events and attitudes of his own time. Contemporary audiences have all but lost sight of the scandal that was a backdrop for the play: the Gunpowder Plot of 1605, in which several Catholic zealots plotted to blow up King James I and his Protestant Parliament. Garry Wills, a professor and political columnist, says that for its Elizabethan audience, *Macbeth* was a thriller. (For Wills, the Gunpowder Plot would compare to a plan to bomb the U.S. Capitol building during a presidential address.) The threat to an anointed king, and the perceived evil behind it, was relived in Macbeth's threat to the social order in a Scotland of the distant past.

Shakespeare altered his source text, in ways both small and large, in order to pay homage to his own king and country; his changes were intended for an audience of his *particular* moment in history. If he ever saw it, *Macbeth* must have pleased King James, the patron of Shakespeare's company. Since James had recently survived the Gunpowder Plot, he was especially interested in attacks on kings. James always defended the idea that he ruled by divine right. Moreover, he was a Scot and claimed to be a direct descendant of Banquo, to whom the third witch says, "Thou shalt get kings, though thou be none." For these reasons, scholars have for a long time thought of *Macbeth* as a play written for a command performance at court, though there is absolutely no proof that it was. James refused to sit through long plays, and this royal shortcoming has even been used to explain the fact that *Macbeth* is one of Shakespeare's shortest plays.

We can also say that Shakespeare made many changes to Holinshed's story because he was much more interested in psychological truth than in historical fact. And in this sense, *Macbeth* is also about *real* people, men and women tempted by ambition and power, caught up in a web of wants and needs. In playing out these real feelings and desires, Shakespeare's Macbeth transcends the historical Macbeth and gives us a portrait and a play for all time. As the critic Sylvan Barnet notes, "When one reads or sees *Macbeth,* one cannot help feeling that one is experiencing a re-creation or representation of what a man is, in the present, even in the timeless."

The Tragedy of Macbeth

by
William Shakespeare

Characters

DUNCAN, king of Scotland

MALCOLM
DONALBAIN
} his sons

MACBETH
BANQUO
MACDUFF
LENNOX
ROSS
MENTEITH
ANGUS
CAITHNESS
} noblemen of Scotland

FLEANCE, son to Banquo

SIWARD, earl of Northumberland, general of the English forces

YOUNG SIWARD, his son

SEYTON, an officer attending on Macbeth

SON to Macduff

AN ENGLISH DOCTOR

A SCOTTISH DOCTOR

A PORTER

AN OLD MAN

THREE MURDERERS

LADY MACBETH

LADY MACDUFF

A GENTLEWOMAN attending on Lady Macbeth

HECATE

WITCHES

APPARITIONS

LORDS, OFFICERS, SOLDIERS, ATTENDANTS, and MESSENGERS

Setting: Scotland; England

Act I

Scene 1. *An open place.*

Thunder and lightning. Enter three WITCHES.

First Witch.
   When shall we three meet again?
   In thunder, lightning, or in rain?
Second Witch.
   When the hurlyburly's done,
   When the battle's lost and won.
Third Witch.
   That will be ere the set of sun.   5
First Witch.
   Where the place?
Second Witch.   Upon the heath.
Third Witch.
   There to meet with Macbeth.
First Witch.
   I come, Graymalkin.°
Second Witch.
   Paddock° calls.
Third Witch.   Anon!°
All.
   Fair is foul, and foul is fair.   10
   Hover through the fog and filthy air.   [*Exeunt.*]

I.1.8. **Graymalkin:** the witches' attendant, a gray cat.
   9. Paddock: a toad. **Anon!:** Soon!

Scene 2. *A camp.*

Alarum within.° Enter KING DUNCAN, MALCOLM,
DONALBAIN, LENNOX, *with* ATTENDANTS, *meeting a
bleeding* CAPTAIN.

King.
    What bloody man is that? He can report,
    As seemeth by his plight, of the revolt
    The newest state.
Malcolm.   This is the sergeant
    Who like a good and hardy soldier fought
    'Gainst my captivity. Hail, brave friend!   5
    Say to the king the knowledge of the broil°
    As thou didst leave it.
Captain.   Doubtful it stood,
    As two spent swimmers, that do cling together
    And choke their art.° The merciless Macdonwald—
    Worthy to be a rebel for to that   10
    The multiplying villainies of nature
    Do swarm upon him—from the Western Isles°
    Of kerns and gallowglasses° is supplied;
    And Fortune, on his damnèd quarrel smiling,
    Showed like a rebel's whore: but all's too weak: 15
    For brave Macbeth—well he deserves that name—
    Disdaining Fortune, with his brandished steel,
    Which smoked with bloody execution,
    Like valor's minion° carved out his passage
    Till he faced the slave;   20
    Which nev'r shook hands, nor bade farewell to him,

---

s.d. Alarum within: trumpets offstage.
I.2.6. broil: quarrel.
   9. choke their art: hinder each other's ability to swim.
  12. Western Isles: region of West Scotland comprising the Outer Hebrides.
  13. kerns and gallowglasses: lightly armed Irish soldiers and heavily
        armed soldiers.
  19. minion: favorite.

Till he unseamed him from the nave to th' chops,°
And fixed his head upon our battlements.

King.

O valiant cousin! Worthy gentleman!

Captain.

As whence the sun 'gins his reflection°   25
Shipwracking storms and direful thunders break,
So from that spring whence comfort seemed to come
Discomfort swells. Mark, King of Scotland, mark:
No sooner justice had, with valor armed,
Compelled these skipping kerns to trust their heels   30
But the Norweyan° lord, surveying vantage,°
With furbished arms and new supplies of men,
Began a fresh assault.

King.   Dismayed not this
Our captains, Macbeth and Banquo?

Captain.   Yes;
As° sparrows eagles, or the hare the lion.   35
If I say sooth,° I must report they were
As cannons overcharged with double cracks;
So they doubly redoubled strokes upon the foe.
Except° they meant to bathe in reeking wounds,
Or memorize another Golgotha,°   40
I cannot tell—
But I am faint; my gashes cry for help.

King.

So well thy words become thee as thy wounds;
They smack of honor both. Go get him surgeons.

Exit CAPTAIN *attended.*

---

22. **unseamed . . . chops:** split him from navel to jaws.
25. **'gins his reflection:** rises.
31. **Norweyan:** Norwegian. **surveying vantage:** seeing an opportunity.
35. **As:** no more than.
36. **sooth:** truth.
39. **Except:** unless.
40. **memorize another Golgotha:** make the place as memorable as Golgotha, where Christ was crucified.

Enter ROSS *and* ANGUS.

> Who comes here?
> **Malcolm.** The worthy Thane° of Ross. 45
> **Lennox.**
> What a haste looks through his eyes! So should he look
> That seems to° speak things strange.
> **Ross.** God save the king!
> **King.**
> Whence cam'st thou, worthy thane?
> **Ross.** From Fife, great king;
> Where the Norweyan banners flout the sky
> And fan our people cold. 50
> Norway himself,° with terrible numbers,
> Assisted by that most disloyal traitor
> The Thane of Cawdor, began a dismal conflict;
> Till that Bellona's bridegroom,° lapped in proof,°
> Confronted him with self-comparisons,° 55
> Point against point, rebellious arm 'gainst arm,
> Curbing his lavish° spirit: and, to conclude,
> The victory fell on us.
> **King.** Great happiness!
> **Ross.** That now
> Sweno, the Norways' king, craves composition;°
> Nor would we deign him burial of his men 60
> Till he disbursèd, at Saint Colme's Inch,°
> Ten thousand dollars to our general use.

---

45. **Thane:** Scottish title of nobility.
47. **seems to:** seems about to.
51. **Norway himself:** that is, the king of Norway.
54. **Bellona's bridegroom:** Bellona is the goddess of war. Macbeth, who is a great soldier, is called her mate. **lapped in proof:** clad in armor.
55. **self-comparisons:** countermovements.
57. **lavish:** insolent; rude.
59. **composition:** peace terms.
61. **Saint Colme's Inch:** island off the coast of Scotland.

King.

No more that Thane of Cawdor shall deceive
Our bosom interest:° go pronounce his present° death,
And with his former title greet Macbeth.   65

Ross.

I'll see it done.

King.

What he hath lost, noble Macbeth hath won.   [*Exeunt.*]

Scene 3. *A heath.*

Thunder. Enter the three WITCHES.

First Witch.

Where hast thou been, sister?

Second Witch.

Killing swine.

Third Witch.

Sister, where thou?

First Witch.

A sailor's wife had chestnuts in her lap,
And mounched, and mounched, and mounched.
    "Give me," quoth I.   5
"Aroint thee,° witch!" the rump-fed ronyon° cries.
Her husband's to Aleppo gone, master o' th' *Tiger:*
But in a sieve° I'll thither sail,
And, like a rat without a tail,
I'll do, I'll do, and I'll do.   10

Second Witch.

I'll give thee a wind.

First Witch.

Th' art kind.

---

64. **bosom interest:** heart's trust. **present:** immediate.
I.3.6. **Aroint thee:** begone. **rump-fed ronyon:** fat-rumped, scabby creature.
  8. **But . . . sieve:** Witches were believed to have the power to sail in sieves.

Third Witch.

    And I another.

First Witch.

    I myself have all the other;

    And the very ports they blow,°   15

    All the quarters that they know

    I' th' shipman's card.°

    I'll drain him dry as hay:

    Sleep shall neither night nor day

    Hang upon his penthouse lid;°   20

    He shall live a man forbid:°

    Weary sev'nights nine times nine

    Shall he dwindle, peak,° and pine:

    Though his bark cannot be lost,

    Yet it shall be tempest-tossed.   25

    Look what I have.

Second Witch.

    Show me, show me.

First Witch.

    Here I have a pilot's thumb,

    Wracked as homeward he did come.

Drum within.

Third Witch.

    A drum, a drum!   30

    Macbeth doth come.

All.

    The weird sisters, hand in hand,

    Posters° of the sea and land,

    Thus do go about, about:

    Thrice to thine, and thrice to mine,   35

---

15. **ports they blow:** harbors they blow into.
17. **card:** compass.
20. **penthouse lid:** eyelid.
21. **forbid:** cursed.
23. **peak:** grow pale.
33. **Posters:** travelers.

And thrice again, to make up nine.
Peace! The charm's wound up.

Enter MACBETH *and* BANQUO.

Macbeth.
So foul and fair a day I have not seen.
Banquo.
How far is't called to Forres?° What are these
So withered, and so wild in their attire,   40
That look not like th' inhabitants o' th' earth,
And yet are on't? Live you, or are you aught
That man may question? You seem to understand me,
By each at once her choppy° finger laying
Upon her skinny lips. You should° be women,   45
And yet your beards forbid me to interpret
That you are so.
Macbeth.   Speak, if you can: what are you?
First Witch.
All hail, Macbeth! Hail to thee, Thane of Glamis!
Second Witch.
All hail, Macbeth! Hail to thee, Thane of Cawdor!
Third Witch.
All hail, Macbeth, that shalt be king hereafter!   50
Banquo.
Good sir, why do you start, and seem to fear
Things that do sound so fair? I' th' name of truth,
Are ye fantastical, or that indeed
Which outwardly ye show? My noble partner
You greet with present grace and great prediction   55
Of noble having and of royal hope,
That he seems rapt withal:° to me you speak not.
If you can look into the seeds of time,

---

39. **Forres:** a town in northeast Scotland and site of King Duncan's castle.
44. **choppy:** chapped; sore.
45. **should:** must.
57. **rapt withal:** entranced by it.

And say which grain will grow and which will not,
Speak then to me, who neither beg nor fear   60
Your favors nor your hate.

First Witch. Hail!

Second Witch. Hail!

Third Witch. Hail!

First Witch.

Lesser than Macbeth, and greater.   65

Second Witch.

Not so happy,° yet much happier.

Third Witch.

Thou shalt get° kings, though thou be none.
So all hail, Macbeth and Banquo!

First Witch.

Banquo and Macbeth, all hail!

Macbeth.

Stay, you imperfect° speakers, tell me more: 70
By Sinel's death I know I am Thane of Glamis;
But how of Cawdor? The Thane of Cawdor lives,
A prosperous gentleman; and to be king
Stands not within the prospect of belief,
No more than to be Cawdor. Say from whence   75
You owe° this strange intelligence?° Or why
Upon this blasted heath you stop our way
With such prophetic greeting? Speak, I charge you.

                                        WITCHES *vanish.*

Banquo.

The earth hath bubbles as the water has,
And these are of them. Whither are they vanished?   80

Macbeth.

Into the air, and what seemed corporal° melted
As breath into the wind. Would they had stayed!

---

66. **happy:** lucky.
67. **get:** beget.
70. **imperfect:** incomplete.
76. **owe:** own; have. **intelligence:** information.
81. **corporal:** corporeal (bodily, physical).

Banquo.
> Were such things here as we do speak about?
> Or have we eaten on the insane root°
> That takes the reason prisoner?   85
Macbeth.
> Your children shall be kings.
Banquo.   You shall be king.
Macbeth.
> And Thane of Cawdor too. Went it not so?
Banquo.
> To th' selfsame tune and words. Who's here?

Enter ROSS *and* ANGUS.

Ross.
> The king hath happily received, Macbeth,
> The news of thy success; and when he reads°   90
> Thy personal venture in the rebels' fight,
> His wonders and his praises do contend
> Which should be thine or his. Silenced with that,
> In viewing o'er the rest o' th' selfsame day,
> He finds thee in the stout Norweyan ranks,   95
> Nothing afeard of what thyself didst make,
> Strange images of death.° As thick as tale
> Came post with post,° and every one did bear
> Thy praises in his kingdom's great defense,
> And poured them down before him.
Angus.   We are sent   100
> To give thee, from our royal master, thanks;
> Only to herald thee into his sight,
> Not pay thee.
Ross.
> And for an earnest° of a greater honor,
> He bade me, from him, call thee Thane of Cawdor;   105

---

84. **insane root:** henbane, believed to cause insanity.
90. **reads:** considers.
97. **Nothing ... death:** killing, and not being afraid of being killed.
98. **post with post:** messenger with a message.
104. **earnest:** pledge.

In which addition,° hail, most worthy thane!
For it is thine.
Banquo.   What, can the devil speak true?
Macbeth.
The Thane of Cawdor lives: why do you dress me
In borrowed robes?
Angus.   Who was the thane lives yet,
But under heavy judgment bears that life   110
Which he deserves to lose. Whether he was combined
With those of Norway, or did line° the rebel
With hidden help and vantage, or that with both
He labored in his country's wrack, I know not;
But treasons capital,° confessed and proved,   115
Have overthrown him.
Macbeth (*aside*).   Glamis, and Thane of Cawdor:
The greatest is behind. (*To* ROSS *and* ANGUS.) Thanks
    for your pains.
(*Aside to* BANQUO.) Do you not hope your children
    shall be kings,
When those that gave the Thane of Cawdor to me
Promised no less to them?
Banquo (*aside to* MACBETH). That, trusted home,°   120
Might yet enkindle you unto the crown,°
Besides the Thane of Cawdor. But 'tis strange:
And oftentimes, to win us to our harm,
The instruments of darkness tell us truths,
Win us with honest trifles, to betray's   125
In deepest consequence.
Cousins,° a word, I pray you.
Macbeth (*aside*).   Two truths are told
As happy prologues to the swelling act

---

106. **addition:** title.
112. **line:** support.
115. **capital:** deserving death.
120. **home:** all the way.
121. **enkindle . . . crown:** arouse in you the ambition to become king.
127. **Cousins:** This word is used frequently by Shakespeare to mean
       "fellows" or "kindred friends" of some sort.

Of the imperial theme.—I thank you, gentlemen.—
(*Aside.*) This supernatural soliciting   130
Cannot be ill, cannot be good. If ill,
Why hath it given me earnest of success,
Commencing in a truth? I am Thane of Cawdor:
If good, why do I yield to that suggestion
Whose horrid image doth unfix my hair   135
And make my seated heart knock at my ribs,
Against the use of nature? Present fears
Are less than horrible imaginings.
My thought, whose murder yet is but fantastical,
Shakes so my single° state of man that function   140
Is smothered in surmise, and nothing is
But what is not.°
Banquo.   Look, how our partner's rapt.
Macbeth (*aside*).
   If chance will have me king, why, chance may
      crown me,
   Without my stir.
Banquo.   New honors come upon him,
   Like our strange° garments, cleave not to their mold   145
   But with the aid of use.
Macbeth (*aside*).   Come what come may,
   Time and the hour runs through the roughest day.
Banquo.
   Worthy Macbeth, we stay upon your leisure.
Macbeth.
   Give me your favor.° My dull brain was wrought
   With things forgotten. Kind gentlemen, your pains   150
   Are registered where every day I turn
   The leaf to read them. Let us toward the king.
   (*Aside to* BANQUO.) Think upon what hath chanced,
      and at more time,

---

140. **single:** unaided; weak.
142. **nothing . . . not:** Nothing is real to me except my imaginings.
145. **strange:** new.
149. **favor:** pardon.

The interim having weighed it, let us speak
Our free hearts each to other.

Banquo.   Very gladly.   155

Macbeth.

Till then, enough. Come, friends.   [*Exeunt.*]

Scene 4. *Forres. The palace.*

Flourish.° Enter KING DUNCAN, LENNOX, MALCOLM,
DONALBAIN, *and* ATTENDANTS.

King.

Is execution done on Cawdor? Are not
Those in commission yet returned?

Malcolm.   My liege,

They are not yet come back. But I have spoke
With one that saw him die, who did report
That very frankly he confessed his treasons,   5
Implored your highness' pardon and set forth
A deep repentance: nothing in his life
Became him like the leaving it. He died
As one that had been studied in his death
To throw away the dearest thing he owed°   10
As 'twere a careless trifle.

King.   There's no art

To find the mind's construction in the face:
He was a gentleman on whom I built
An absolute trust.

Enter MACBETH, BANQUO, ROSS, *and* ANGUS.

                    O worthiest cousin!

The sin of my ingratitude even now   15

---

s.d. **Flourish:** of trumpets.
I.4.10. **owed:** owned.

Was heavy on me: thou art so far before,
That swiftest wing of recompense is slow
To overtake thee. Would thou hadst less deserved,
That the proportion° both of thanks and payment
Might have been mine! Only I have left to say,   20
More is thy due than more than all can pay.

Macbeth.

The service and the loyalty I owe,
In doing it, pays itself.° Your highness' part
Is to receive our duties: and our duties
Are to your throne and state children and servants;   25
Which do but what they should, by doing everything
Safe toward° your love and honor.

King.   Welcome hither.

I have begun to plant thee, and will labor
To make thee full of growing. Noble Banquo,
That hast no less deserved, nor must be known   30
No less to have done so, let me enfold thee
And hold thee to my heart.

Banquo.   There if I grow,

The harvest is your own.

King.   My plenteous joys,

Wanton in fullness, seek to hide themselves
In drops of sorrow. Sons, kinsmen, thanes,   35
And you whose places are the nearest, know,
We will establish our estate upon
Our eldest, Malcolm, whom we name hereafter
The Prince of Cumberland: which honor must
Not unaccompanied invest him only,   40
But signs of nobleness, like stars, shall shine
On all deservers. From hence to Inverness,°
And bind us further to you.

---

19. **proportion:** greater amount.
23. **pays itself:** is its own reward.
27. **Safe toward:** safeguarding.
42. **Inverness:** Macbeth's castle.

Macbeth.
　　The rest is labor, which is not used for you.°
　　I'll be myself the harbinger,° and make joyful　　　　45
　　The hearing of my wife with your approach;
　　So, humbly take my leave.
King.　　　　　　　　　　My worthy Cawdor!
Macbeth (*aside*).
　　The Prince of Cumberland! That is a step
　　On which I must fall down, or else o'erleap,
　　For in my way it lies. Stars, hide your fires;　　　　50
　　Let not light see my black and deep desires:
　　The eye wink at the hand;° yet let that be
　　Which the eye fears, when it is done, to see.　　[*Exit.*]
King.
　　True, worthy Banquo; he is full so valiant,
　　And in his commendations° I am fed;　　　　　　55
　　It is a banquet to me. Let's after him,
　　Whose care is gone before to bid us welcome.
　　It is a peerless kinsman.　　　　[*Flourish. Exeunt.*]

Scene 5. *Inverness. Macbeth's castle.*

Enter Macbeth's wife, LADY MACBETH, *alone, with a letter.*

Lady Macbeth (*reads*). "They met me in the day of success;
　　and I have learned by the perfect'st report they have
　　more in them than mortal knowledge. When I burned
　　in desire to question them further, they made them-
　　selves air, into which they vanished. Whiles I stood　　5
　　rapt in the wonder of it, came missives° from the King,
　　who all-hailed me 'Thane of Cawdor'; by which title,
　　before, these weird sisters saluted me, and referred me

---

44. **The rest . . . you:** When rest is not used for you, it is labor.
45. **harbinger:** sign of something to come.
52. **wink . . . hand:** be blind to the hand's deed.
55. **his commendations:** praises of him.
I.5.6. **missives:** messengers.

to the coming on of time, with 'Hail, king that shalt
be!' This have I thought good to deliver thee, my dear- 10
est partner of greatness, that thou mightst not lose the
dues of rejoicing, by being ignorant of what greatness
is promised thee. Lay it to thy heart, and farewell."
Glamis thou art, and Cawdor, and shalt be
What thou art promised. Yet do I fear thy nature; 15
It is too full o' th' milk of human kindness
To catch the nearest way. Thou wouldst be great,
Art not without ambition, but without
The illness° should attend it. What thou wouldst
    highly,
That wouldst thou holily; wouldst not play false, 20
And yet wouldst wrongly win. Thou'dst have,
    great Glamis,
That which cries, "Thus thou must do" if thou have it;
And that which rather thou dost fear to do
Than wishest should be undone. Hie thee hither,
That I may pour my spirits in thine ear, 25
And chastise with the valor of my tongue
All that impedes thee from the golden round
Which fate and metaphysical° aid doth seem
To have thee crowned withal.

Enter MESSENGER.

                              What is your tidings?
Messenger.
    The king comes here tonight.
Lady Macbeth.   Thou'rt mad to say it! 30
    Is not thy master with him, who, were't so,
    Would have informed for preparation?
Messenger.
    So please you, it is true. Our thane is coming.
    One of my fellows had the speed of him,°

---

19. **illness:** wickedness; evil nature.
28. **metaphysical:** supernatural.
34. **had . . . him:** had more speed than he did.

Who, almost dead for breath, had scarcely more   35
Than would make up his message.
Lady Macbeth.   Give him tending;
  He brings great news.   [*Exit* MESSENGER.]
                 The raven himself is hoarse
That croaks the fatal entrance of Duncan
Under my battlements. Come, you spirits
That tend on mortal° thoughts, unsex me here,   40
And fill me, from the crown to the toe, top-full
Of direst cruelty! Make thick my blood,
Stop up th' access and passage to remorse,
That no compunctious visitings of nature°
Shake my fell° purpose, nor keep peace between   45
Th' effect and it! Come to my woman's breasts,
And take my milk for gall,° you murd'ring ministers,°
Wherever in your sightless° substances
You wait on nature's mischief! Come, thick night,
And pall° thee in the dunnest° smoke of hell,   50
That my keen knife see not the wound it makes,
Nor heaven peep through the blanket of the dark,
To cry "Hold, hold!"

Enter MACBETH.

                 Great Glamis! Worthy Cawdor!
Greater than both, by the all-hail hereafter!
Thy letters have transported me beyond   55
This ignorant present, and I feel now
The future in the instant.
Macbeth.   My dearest love,
  Duncan comes here tonight.
Lady Macbeth.   And when goes hence?

---

40. **mortal:** deadly.
44. **compunctious . . . nature:** natural feelings of compassion.
45. **fell:** savage.
47. **gall:** a bitter substance; bile. **murd'ring ministers:** agents of murder.
48. **sightless:** invisible.
50. **pall:** cover with a shroud, a burial cloth. **dunnest:** darkest.

Macbeth.

Tomorrow, as he purposes.

Lady Macbeth.   O, never

Shall sun that morrow see!   60

Your face, my thane, is as a book where men

May read strange matters. To beguile the time,°

Look like the time; bear welcome in your eye,

Your hand, your tongue: look like th' innocent flower,

But be the serpent under't. He that's coming   65

Must be provided for: and you shall put

This night's great business into my dispatch;°

Which shall to all our nights and days to come

Give solely sovereign sway and masterdom.

Macbeth.

We will speak further.

Lady Macbeth.   Only look up clear.°   70

To alter favor ever is to fear.°

Leave all the rest to me.   [*Exeunt.*]

Scene 6. *Before Macbeth's castle.*

Hautboys° and torches. Enter KING DUNCAN, MALCOLM,
DONALBAIN, BANQUO, LENNOX, MACDUFF, ROSS, ANGUS,
and ATTENDANTS.

King.

This castle hath a pleasant seat;° the air

Nimbly and sweetly recommends itself

Unto our gentle senses.

---

62. **beguile the time:** deceive people of the day.

67. **dispatch:** management.

70. **clear:** undisturbed.

71. **To alter . . . fear:** To show an altered face is dangerous.

s.d. **Hautboys:** oboes.

I.6.1. **seat:** situation; setting.

Banquo.   This guest of summer,
   The temple-haunting martlet,° does approve°
   By his loved mansionry° that the heaven's breath   5
   Smells wooingly here. No jutty,° frieze,
   Buttress, nor coign of vantage,° but this bird
   Hath made his pendent bed and procreant° cradle.
   Where they most breed and haunt, I have observed
   The air is delicate.

Enter LADY MACBETH.

King.   See, see, our honored hostess!   10
   The love that follows us sometime is our trouble,
   Which still we thank as love. Herein I teach you
   How you shall bid God 'ield° us for your pains
   And thank us for your trouble.
Lady Macbeth.   All our service
   In every point twice done, and then done double,   15
   Were poor and single business to contend
   Against those honors deep and broad wherewith
   Your majesty loads our house: for those of old,
   And the late dignities heaped up to them,
   We rest your hermits.°
King.   Where's the Thane of Cawdor?   20
   We coursed° him at the heels, and had a purpose
   To be his purveyor:° but he rides well,
   And his great love, sharp as his spur, hath holp° him
   To his home before us. Fair and noble hostess,
   We are your guest tonight.

---

   4. **martlet:** a bird that builds nests in churches. **approve:** prove.
   5. **mansionry:** nest (dwelling).
   6. **jutty:** projection.
   7. **coign of vantage:** advantageous corner (of the castle).
   8. **procreant:** breeding.
  13. **'ield:** reward.
  20. **We rest your hermits:** We'll remain dependents who will pray for you.
  21. **coursed:** chased.
  22. **purveyor:** advance man.
  23. **holp:** helped.

Lady Macbeth.   Your servants ever   25
    Have theirs, themselves, and what is theirs, in compt,°
    To make their audit at your highness' pleasure,
    Still° to return your own.
King.   Give me your hand.
    Conduct me to mine host: we love him highly,
    And shall continue our graces toward him.   30
    By your leave, hostess.   [*Exeunt.*]

Scene 7. *Macbeth's castle.*

Hautboys. Torches. Enter a SEWER,° *and diverse* SERVANTS
with dishes and service, and pass over the stage. Then enter
MACBETH.

Macbeth.
    If it were done when 'tis done, then 'twere well
    It were done quickly. If th' assassination
    Could trammel up the consequence, and catch,
    With his surcease,° success; that but this blow
    Might be the be-all and the end-all—here,   5
    But here, upon this bank and shoal of time,
    We'd jump° the life to come. But in these cases
    We still have judgment here; that we but teach
    Bloody instructions, which, being taught, return
    To plague th' inventor: this even-handed° justice   10
    Commends° th' ingredients of our poisoned chalice
    To our own lips. He's here in double trust:

---

26. **in compt:** in trust.
28. **Still:** always.
s.d. **Sewer:** butler.
I.7.4. **his surcease:** Duncan's death.
  7. **jump:** risk. (Macbeth knows he will be condemned to Hell for the sin of murder.)
10. **even-handed:** impartial.
11. **Commends:** offers.

First, as I am his kinsman and his subject,
Strong both against the deed; then, as his host,
Who should against his murderer shut the door,   15
Not bear the knife myself. Besides, this Duncan
Hath borne his faculties° so meek, hath been
So clear° in his great office, that his virtues
Will plead like angels trumpet-tongued against
The deep damnation of his taking-off;°   20
And pity, like a naked newborn babe,
Striding the blast, or heaven's cherubin horsed
Upon the sightless couriers° of the air,
Shall blow the horrid deed in every eye,
That° tears shall drown the wind. I have no spur   25
To prick the sides of my intent, but only
Vaulting ambition, which o'erleaps itself
And falls on th' other——

Enter LADY MACBETH.

                              How now! What news?
Lady Macbeth.
    He has almost supped. Why have you left the
        chamber?
Macbeth.
    Hath he asked for me?
Lady Macbeth.   Know you not he has?   30
Macbeth.
    We will proceed no further in this business:
    He hath honored me of late, and I have bought
    Golden opinions from all sorts of people,
    Which would be worn now in their newest gloss,
    Not cast aside so soon.
Lady Macbeth.   Was the hope drunk   35
    Wherein you dressed yourself? Hath it slept since?

---

17. **faculties:** powers.
18. **clear:** clean.
20. **taking-off:** murder.
23. **sightless couriers:** winds.
25. **That:** so that.

And wakes it now, to look so green° and pale
At what it did so freely? From this time
Such I account thy love. Art thou afeard
To be the same in thine own act and valor   40
As thou art in desire? Wouldst thou have that
Which thou esteem'st the ornament of life,°
And live a coward in thine own esteem,
Letting "I dare not" wait upon° "I would,"
Like the poor cat i' th' adage?°

Macbeth.   Prithee, peace!   45
I dare do all that may become a man;
Who dares do more is none.

Lady Macbeth.   What beast was't then
That made you break° this enterprise to me?
When you durst do it, then you were a man;
And to be more than what you were, you would   50
Be so much more the man. Nor time nor place
Did then adhere,° and yet you would make both.
They have made themselves, and that their fitness
      now
Does unmake you. I have given suck, and know
How tender 'tis to love the babe that milks me: 55
I would, while it was smiling in my face,
Have plucked my nipple from his boneless gums,
And dashed the brains out, had I so sworn as you
Have done to this.

Macbeth.   If we should fail?

Lady Macbeth.   We fail?
But° screw your courage to the sticking-place,°   60
And we'll not fail. When Duncan is asleep—

---

37. **green:** sickly.
42. **ornament of life:** crown.
44. **wait upon:** follow.
45. **poor . . . adage:** reference to a saying about a cat who wants fish but won't wet its paws.
48. **break:** disclose; reveal.
52. **adhere:** suit.
60. **But:** only. **sticking-place:** the notch in a crossbow.

Whereto the rather shall his day's hard journey
Soundly invite him—his two chamberlains
Will I with wine and wassail° so convince,°
That memory, the warder of the brain,   65
Shall be a fume, and the receipt of reason
A limbeck only:° when in swinish sleep
Their drenchèd natures lie as in a death,
What cannot you and I perform upon
Th' unguarded Duncan, what not put upon   70
His spongy officers, who shall bear the guilt
Of our great quell?

Macbeth.   Bring forth men-children only;
For thy undaunted mettle° should compose
Nothing but males. Will it not be received,
When we have marked with blood those sleepy two   75
Of his own chamber, and used their very daggers,
That they have done't?

Lady Macbeth.   Who dares receive it other,
As we shall make our griefs and clamor roar
Upon his death?

Macbeth.   I am settled, and bend up
Each corporal agent to this terrible feat.   80
Away, and mock the time° with fairest show:
False face must hide what the false heart doth know.

Exeunt.

---

64. **wassail:** drinking. **convince:** overcome.
67. **the receipt . . . only:** The reasoning part of the brain would become
like a **limbeck** (or still), distilling only confused thoughts.
73. **mettle:** spirit.
81. **mock the time:** deceive the world.

Act II

Scene 1. *Inverness. Court of Macbeth's castle.*

Enter BANQUO, *and* FLEANCE, *with a torch before him (on the way to bed).*

Banquo.
How goes the night, boy?

Fleance.
The moon is down; I have not heard the clock.

Banquo.
And she goes down at twelve.

Fleance.   I take't, 'tis later, sir.

Banquo.
Hold, take my sword. There's husbandry° in heaven.
Their candles are all out. Take thee that too.   5
A heavy summons° lies like lead upon me,
And yet I would not sleep. Merciful powers,
Restrain in me the cursèd thoughts that nature
Gives way to in repose!

Enter MACBETH, *and a* SERVANT *with a torch.*

                          Give me my sword!
Who's there?   10

Macbeth.
A friend.

Banquo.
What, sir, not yet at rest? The king's a-bed:
He hath been in unusual pleasure, and
Sent forth great largess to your offices:°

II.1.4. **husbandry:** economizing.
  6. **summons:** call to sleep.
  14. **largess to your offices:** gifts to your servants' quarters.

This diamond he greets your wife withal,   15
By the name of most kind hostess; and shut up°
In measureless content.
Macbeth.   Being unprepared,
Our will became the servant to defect,°
Which else should free have wrought.
Banquo.   All's well.
I dreamt last night of the three weird sisters: 20
To you they have showed some truth.
Macbeth.   I think not of them.
Yet, when we can entreat an hour to serve,
We would spend it in some words upon that business,
If you would grant the time.
Banquo.   At your kind'st leisure.
Macbeth.
If you shall cleave to my consent, when 'tis,°   25
It shall make honor for you.
Banquo.   So° I lose none
In seeking to augment it, but still keep
My bosom franchised° and allegiance clear,°
I shall be counseled.
Macbeth.   Good repose the while!
Banquo.
Thanks, sir. The like to you!   30

Exit BANQUO, *with* FLEANCE.

Macbeth.
Go bid thy mistress, when my drink is ready,
She strike upon the bell. Get thee to bed.

Exit SERVANT.

Is this a dagger which I see before me,
The handle toward my hand? Come, let me clutch thee.

---

16. **shut up:** concluded.
18. **defect:** insufficient preparations.
25. **cleave . . . 'tis:** join my cause, when the time comes.
26. **So:** provided that.
28. **franchised:** free (from guilt). **clear:** clean.

I have thee not, and yet I see thee still.   35
Art thou not, fatal vision, sensible°
To feeling as to sight, or art thou but
A dagger of the mind, a false creation,
Proceeding from the heat-oppressèd brain?
I see thee yet, in form as palpable°   40
As this which now I draw.
Thou marshal'st me the way that I was going;
And such an instrument I was to use.
Mine eyes are made the fools o' th' other senses,
Or else worth all the rest. I see thee still;   45
And on thy blade and dudgeon° gouts° of blood,
Which was not so before. There's no such thing.
It is the bloody business which informs°
Thus to mine eyes. Now o'er the one half-world
Nature seems dead, and wicked dreams abuse°   50
The curtained sleep; witchcraft celebrates
Pale Hecate's° offerings; and withered murder,
Alarumed° by his sentinel, the wolf,
Whose howl's his watch, thus with his stealthy pace,
With Tarquin's° ravishing strides, towards his design   55
Moves like a ghost. Thou sure and firm-set earth,
Hear not my steps, which way they walk, for fear
Thy very stones prate of my whereabout,
And take the present horror from the time,
Which now suits with it.° Whiles I threat, he lives: 60
Words to the heat of deeds too cold breath gives.

A bell rings.

---

36. **sensible:** perceptible to the senses.
40. **palpable:** obvious.
46. **dudgeon:** hilt. **gouts:** large drops.
48. **informs:** gives shape.
50. **abuse:** deceive.
52. **Hecate's:** Hecate (hek'it) is the goddess of sorcery.
53. **Alarumed:** called to action.
55. **Tarquin's:** Tarquin was a Roman tyrant who raped a woman named Lucrece.
60. **suits with it:** seems suitable to it.

I go, and it is done: the bell invites me.
Hear it not, Duncan, for it is a knell
That summons thee to heaven, or to hell.   [*Exit.*]

Scene 2. *Macbeth's castle.*

Enter LADY MACBETH.

Lady Macbeth.
  That which hath made them drunk hath made me bold;
  What hath quenched them hath given me fire.
    Hark! Peace!
  It was the owl that shrieked, the fatal bellman,
  Which gives the stern'st good-night.° He is about it.
  The doors are open, and the surfeited grooms   5
  Do mock their charge with snores. I have drugged
      their possets,°
  That death and nature do contend about them,
  Whether they live or die.
Macbeth (*within*).   Who's there? What, ho?
Lady Macbeth.
  Alack, I am afraid they have awaked
  And 'tis not done! Th' attempt and not the deed   10
  Confounds° us. Hark! I laid their daggers ready;
  He could not miss 'em. Had he not resembled
  My father as he slept, I had done't.

Enter MACBETH.

                    My husband!
Macbeth.
  I have done the deed. Didst thou not hear a noise?

II.2.4. **stern'st good-night:** The owl's call is supposed to portend death.
    The bellman was a person who rang a bell outside a condemned
    person's cell the night before the execution, to warn the person to
    confess his or her sins.
  6. **possets:** bedtime drinks.
  11. **Confounds:** ruins.

Lady Macbeth.
 I heard the owl scream and the crickets cry.   15
 Did not you speak?
Macbeth.   When?
Lady Macbeth.   Now.
Macbeth.   As I descended?
Lady Macbeth. Ay.
Macbeth. Hark!
 Who lies i' th' second chamber?
Lady Macbeth.   Donalbain.
Macbeth. This is a sorry sight.   20
Lady Macbeth.
 A foolish thought, to say a sorry sight.
Macbeth.
 There's one did laugh in's sleep, and one cried
  "Murder!"
 That they did wake each other. I stood and heard them.
 But they did say their prayers, and addressed them
 Again to sleep.
Lady Macbeth. There are two lodged together. 25
Macbeth.
 One cried "God bless us!" and "Amen" the other,
 As they had seen me with these hangman's hands:
 List'ning their fear, I could not say "Amen,"
 When they did say "God bless us!"
Lady Macbeth.   Consider it not so deeply.
Macbeth.
 But wherefore could not I pronounce "Amen"? 30
 I had most need of blessing, and "Amen"
 Stuck in my throat.
Lady Macbeth. These deeds must not be thought
 After these ways; so, it will make us mad.
Macbeth.
 Methought I heard a voice cry "Sleep no more!
 Macbeth does murder sleep"—the innocent sleep, 35
 Sleep that knits up the raveled sleave° of care,

---

36. **raveled sleave:** tangled thread.

The death of each day's life, sore labor's bath,
Balm of hurt minds, great nature's second course,°
Chief nourisher in life's feast——
Lady Macbeth.   What do you mean?
Macbeth.
    Still it cried "Sleep no more!" to all the house: 40
    "Glamis hath murdered sleep, and therefore Cawdor
    Shall sleep no more: Macbeth shall sleep no more."
Lady Macbeth.
    Who was it that thus cried? Why, worthy thane,
    You do unbend your noble strength, to think
    So brainsickly of things. Go get some water,   45
    And wash this filthy witness from your hand.
    Why did you bring these daggers from the place?
    They must lie there: go carry them, and smear
    The sleepy grooms with blood.
Macbeth.   I'll go no more.
    I am afraid to think what I have done;   50
    Look on't again I dare not.
Lady Macbeth.   Infirm of purpose!
    Give me the daggers. The sleeping and the dead
    Are but as pictures. 'Tis the eye of childhood
    That fears a painted devil. If he do bleed,
    I'll gild the faces of the grooms withal,   55
    For it must seem their guilt.   [*Exit. Knock within.*]
Macbeth.   Whence is that knocking?
    How is't with me, when every noise appalls me?
    What hands are here? Ha! They pluck out mine eyes!
    Will all great Neptune's ocean wash this blood
    Clean from my hand? No; this my hand will rather   60
    The multitudinous seas incarnadine,°
    Making the green one red.

Enter LADY MACBETH.

---

38. **second course:** sleep (the less substantial first course is food).
61. **incarnadine:** make red.

Lady Macbeth.

My hands are of your color, but I shame

To wear a heart so white. (*Knock.*) I hear a knocking

At the south entry. Retire we to our chamber.   65

A little water clears us of this deed:

How easy is it then! Your constancy

Hath left you unattended.° (*Knock.*) Hark! more
   knocking.

Get on your nightgown, lest occasion call us

And show us to be watchers.° Be not lost   70

So poorly in your thoughts.

Macbeth.

To know my deed, 'twere best not know myself.

Knock.

Wake Duncan with thy knocking! I would thou couldst!

                                        Exeunt.

Scene 3. *Macbeth's castle.*

Enter a PORTER. *Knocking within.*

Porter. Here's a knocking indeed! If a man were porter
of hell gate, he should have old° turning the key.
(*Knock.*) Knock, knock, knock! Who's there, i' th' name
of Beelzebub?° Here's a farmer, that hanged himself
on th' expectation of plenty. Come in time! Have nap-   5
kins enow° about you; here you'll sweat for't. (*Knock.*)
Knock, knock! Who's there, in th' other devil's name?

---

68. **Your . . . unattended:** Your firmness has deserted you.

70. **watchers:** that is, up late.

II.3.2. **have old:** grow old.

4. **Beelzebub:** the Devil.

6. **enow:** enough.

Faith, here's an equivocator,° that could swear in
both the scales against either scale; who committed
treason enough for God's sake, yet could not equiv-   10
ocate to heaven. O, come in, equivocator. (*Knock.*)
Knock, knock, knock! Who's there? Faith, here's an
English tailor come hither for stealing out of a
French hose:° come in, tailor. Here you may roast
your goose.° (*Knock.*) Knock, knock; never at quiet!   15
What are you? But this place is too cold for hell. I'll
devil-porter it no further. I had thought to have let
in some of all professions that go the primrose
way to th' everlasting bonfire. (*Knock.*) Anon, anon!
(*Opens an entrance.*) I pray you, remember the porter.   20

Enter MACDUFF *and* LENNOX.

Macduff.
Was it so late, friend, ere you went to bed,
That you do lie so late?
Porter. Faith, sir, we were carousing till the second cock:°
and drink, sir, is a great provoker of three things.
Macduff. What three things does drink especially provoke?   25
Porter. Marry, sir, nose-painting, sleep, and urine.
Lechery, sir, it provokes and unprovokes; it provokes the desire, but it takes away the performance:
therefore much drink may be said to be an equivocator with lechery: it makes him and it mars him; it   30
sets him on and it takes him off; it persuades him
and disheartens him; makes him stand to and not
stand to; in conclusion, equivocates him in a sleep,
and giving him the lie, leaves him.
Macduff. I believe drink gave thee the lie° last night.   35

---

8. **equivocator:** The porter means a Jesuit (Jesuits were believed to use false arguments in their zeal for souls).
14. **French hose:** tightfitting stocking.
15. **goose:** iron used by a tailor for pressing.
23. **second cock:** about 3:00 A.M.
35. **gave thee the lie:** pun meaning "called you a liar" and "stretched you out, lying in bed."

Porter. That it did, sir, i' the very throat on me: but I
  requited him for his lie, and, I think, being too
  strong for him, though he took up my legs
  sometime, yet I make a shift to cast° him.

Macduff. Is thy master stirring?   40

Enter MACBETH.

  Our knocking has awaked him; here he comes.

Lennox.

  Good morrow, noble sir.

Macbeth.   Good morrow, both.

Macduff.

  Is the king stirring, worthy thane?

Macbeth.   Not yet.

Macduff.

  He did command me to call timely° on him:
  I have almost slipped the hour.

Macbeth.   I'll bring you to him.   45

Macduff.

  I know this is a joyful trouble to you;
  But yet 'tis one.

Macbeth.

  The labor we delight in physics° pain.
  This is the door.

Macduff.   I'll make so bold to call,
  For 'tis my limited service.°   [*Exit* MACDUFF.]   50

Lennox.

  Goes the king hence today?

Macbeth.   He does: he did appoint so.

Lennox.

  The night has been unruly. Where we lay,
  Our chimneys were blown down, and, as they say,
  Lamentings heard i' th' air, strange screams of death,

---

39. **cast:** pun meaning "cast in plaster" and "vomit" (cast out).
44. **timely:** early.
48. **physics:** cures.
50. **limited service:** appointed duty.

And prophesying with accents terrible   55
Of dire combustion° and confused events
New hatched to th' woeful time: the obscure bird
Clamored the livelong night. Some say, the earth
Was feverous and did shake.

Macbeth.   'Twas a rough night.

Lennox.

My young remembrance cannot parallel   60
A fellow to it.

Enter MACDUFF.

Macduff.

O horror, horror, horror! Tongue nor heart
Cannot conceive nor name thee.

Macbeth and Lennox.   What's the matter?

Macduff.

Confusion now hath made his masterpiece.
Most sacrilegious murder hath broke ope   65
The Lord's anointed temple,° and stole thence
The life o' th' building.

Macbeth.   What is't you say? The life?

Lennox.

Mean you his majesty?

Macduff.

Approach the chamber, and destroy your sight
With a new Gorgon:° do not bid me speak;   70
See, and then speak yourselves. Awake, awake!

Exeunt MACBETH *and* LENNOX.

Ring the alarum bell. Murder and treason!
Banquo and Donalbain! Malcolm! Awake!
Shake off this downy sleep, death's counterfeit,
And look on death itself! Up, up, and see   75

---

56. **combustion:** tumult; uproar.
66. **Lord's anointed temple:** body of the king.
70. **Gorgon:** creature from Greek mythology whose face could turn an
onlooker to stone.

The great doom's image! Malcolm! Banquo!
As from your graves rise up, and walk like sprites,
To countenance° this horror. Ring the bell.

Bell rings. Enter LADY MACBETH.

Lady Macbeth.
　What's the business,
　That such a hideous trumpet calls to parley°　　　　　80
　The sleepers of the house? Speak, speak!
Macduff.　　　　　　　　　　O gentle lady,
　'Tis not for you to hear what I can speak:
　The repetition, in a woman's ear,
　Would murder as it fell.

Enter BANQUO.

　　　　　　　　　　O Banquo, Banquo!
　Our royal master's murdered.
Lady Macbeth.　　　　　　Woe, alas!　　　　　85
　What, in our house?
Banquo.　　　　　　Too cruel anywhere.
　Dear Duff, I prithee, contradict thyself,
　And say it is not so.

Enter MACBETH, LENNOX, *and* ROSS.

Macbeth.
　Had I but died an hour before this chance,
　I had lived a blessèd time; for from this instant　　　90
　There's nothing serious in mortality:°
　All is but toys. Renown and grace is dead,
　The wine of life is drawn, and the mere lees°
　Is left this vault° to brag of.

Enter MALCOLM *and* DONALBAIN.

78.　**countenance:** be in keeping with.
80.　**parley:** conference of war.
91.　**mortality:** life.
93.　**lees:** dregs.
94.　**vault:** pun on "wine vault" and the "vault of heaven."

Donalbain.

 What is amiss?

Macbeth.   You are, and do not know't.   95

 The spring, the head, the fountain of your blood

 Is stopped; the very source of it is stopped.

Macduff.

 Your royal father's murdered.

Malcolm.   O, by whom?

Lennox.

 Those of his chamber, as it seemed, had done't:

 Their hands and faces were all badged° with blood; 100

 So were their daggers, which unwiped we found

 Upon their pillows. They stared, and were distracted.

 No man's life was to be trusted with them.

Macbeth.

 O, yet I do repent me of my fury,

 That I did kill them.

Macduff.   Wherefore did you so?   105

Macbeth.

 Who can be wise, amazed, temp'rate and furious,

 Loyal and neutral, in a moment? No man.

 The expedition° of my violent love

 Outrun the pauser, reason. Here lay Duncan,

 His silver skin laced with his golden blood,   110

 And his gashed stabs looked like a breach in nature

 For ruin's wasteful entrance: there, the murderers,

 Steeped in the colors of their trade, their daggers

 Unmannerly breeched with gore.° Who could refrain,°

 That had a heart to love, and in that heart   115

 Courage to make's love known?

Lady Macbeth.   Help me hence, ho!

Macduff.

 Look to the lady.

---

100. **badged:** marked.
108. **expedition:** haste.
114. **Unmannerly breeched with gore:** unbecomingly covered with
  blood, as if wearing red trousers. **refrain:** check oneself.

Malcolm (*aside to* DONALBAIN).
    Why do we hold our tongues,
    That most may claim this argument for ours?°
Donalbain (*aside to* MALCOLM).
    What should be spoken here,   120
    Where our fate, hid in an auger-hole,°
    May rush, and seize us? Let's away:
    Our tears are not yet brewed.
Malcolm (*aside to* DONALBAIN).
    Nor our strong sorrow
    Upon the foot of motion.°
Banquo.   Look to the lady.   125

              LADY MACBETH *is carried out.*

    And when we have our naked frailties hid,°
    That suffer in exposure, let us meet
    And question° this most bloody piece of work,
    To know it further. Fears and scruples° shake us.
    In the great hand of God I stand, and thence   130
    Against the undivulged pretense° I fight
    Of treasonous malice.
Macduff.   And so do I.
All.   So all.
Macbeth.
    Let's briefly° put on manly readiness,
    And meet i' th' hall together.
All.   Well contented.

      Exeunt all but MALCOLM *and* DONALBAIN.

---

119. **That . . . ours:** who are the most concerned with this topic.
121. **auger-hole:** unsuspected place.
125. **Our tears . . . motion:** We have not yet had time to shed tears or to express our sorrows in action.
126. **naked frailties hid:** poor bodies clothed.
128. **question:** discuss.
129. **scruples:** suspicions.
131. **undivulged pretense:** hidden purpose.
133. **briefly:** quickly.

Malcolm.

    What will you do? Let's not consort with them.   135

    To show an unfelt sorrow is an office°

    Which the false man does easy. I'll to England.

Donalbain.

    To Ireland, I; our separated fortune

    Shall keep us both the safer. Where we are

    There's daggers in men's smiles; the near in blood,   140

    The nearer bloody.

Malcolm.   This murderous shaft that's shot

    Hath not yet lighted, and our safest way

    Is to avoid the aim. Therefore to horse;

    And let us not be dainty of° leave-taking,

    But shift away. There's warrant° in that theft   145

    Which steals itself° when there's no mercy left.

Exeunt.

Scene 4. *Outside Macbeth's castle.*

Enter ROSS *with an* OLD MAN.

Old Man.

    Threescore and ten I can remember well:

    Within the volume of which time I have seen

    Hours dreadful and things strange, but this sore° night

    Hath trifled former knowings.°

Ross.   Ha, good father,

    Thou seest the heavens, as troubled with man's act,   5

    Threatens his bloody stage. By th' clock 'tis day,

    And yet dark night strangles the traveling lamp:°

---

136. **office:** function.
144. **dainty of:** fussy about.
145. **warrant:** justification.
146. **steals itself:** steals oneself away.
II.4.3. **sore:** grievous.
   4. **trifled former knowings:** made trifles of earlier experiences.
   7. **traveling lamp:** sun.

Is't night's predominance,° or the day's shame,
That darkness does the face of earth entomb,
When living light should kiss it?

Old Man.   'Tis unnatural,   10
Even like the deed that's done. On Tuesday last
A falcon, tow'ring in her pride of place,°
Was by a mousing° owl hawked at and killed.

Ross.
And Duncan's horses—a thing most strange and
    certain—
Beauteous and swift, the minions° of their race,   15
Turned wild in nature, broke their stalls, flung out,°
Contending 'gainst obedience, as they would make
War with mankind.

Old Man.   'Tis said they eat° each other.

Ross.
They did so, to th' amazement of mine eyes,
That looked upon't.

Enter MACDUFF.

                                    Here comes the good Macduff.   20
How goes the world, sir, now?

Macduff.   Why, see you not?

Ross.
Is't known who did this more than bloody deed?

Macduff.
Those that Macbeth hath slain.

Ross.   Alas, the day!
What good could they pretend?°

Macduff.   They were suborned:°
Malcolm and Donalbain, the king's two sons,   25

---

8. **predominance:** astrological supremacy.
12. **tow'ring . . . place:** soaring at her summit.
13. **mousing:** normally mouse-eating.
15. **minions:** darlings.
16. **flung out:** lunged wildly.
18. **eat:** ate.
24. **pretend:** hope for. **suborned:** bribed.

Are stol'n away and fled, which puts upon them
Suspicion of the deed.

Ross.   'Gainst nature still.
Thriftless° ambition, that will ravin up°
Thine own life's means!° Then 'tis most like
The sovereignty will fall upon Macbeth.   30

Macduff.
He is already named,° and gone to Scone°
To be invested.°

Ross.   Where is Duncan's body?

Macduff.
Carried to Colmekill,°
The sacred storehouse of his predecessors
And guardian of their bones.

Ross.   Will you to Scone?   35

Macduff.
No, cousin, I'll to Fife.

Ross.   Well, I will thither.

Macduff.
Well, may you see things well done there. Adieu,
Lest our old robes sit easier than our new!

Ross.
Farewell, father.

Old Man.
God's benison° go with you, and with those   40
That would make good of bad, and friends of foes!

                                        Exeunt omnes.

---

28. **Thriftless:** wasteful. **ravin up:** greedily devour.
29. **own life's means:** parent.
31. **named:** elected. **Scone** (sko͞on).
32. **invested:** installed as king.
33. **Colmekill:** Iona Island, the ancient burying place of Scottish kings.
    (It was founded by Saint Colm.)
40. **benison:** blessing.

Act III

Scene 1. *Forres. The palace.*

Enter BANQUO.

Banquo.
Thou hast it now: king, Cawdor, Glamis, all,
As the weird women promised, and I fear
Thou play'dst most foully for't. Yet it was said
It should not stand° in thy posterity,
But that myself should be the root and father   5
Of many kings. If there come truth from them—
As upon thee, Macbeth, their speeches shine—
Why, by the verities on thee made good,
May they not be my oracles as well
And set me up in hope? But hush, no more!   10

Sennet° sounded. Enter MACBETH *as king,* LADY MACBETH,
LENNOX, ROSS, LORDS, *and* ATTENDANTS.

Macbeth.
Here's our chief guest.
Lady Macbeth.   If he had been forgotten,
It had been as a gap in our great feast,
And all-thing° unbecoming.
Macbeth.
Tonight we hold a solemn supper, sir,
And I'll request your presence.
Banquo.   Let your highness   15
Command upon me, to the which my duties

III.1.4.   **stand:** continue.
  s.d.   **Sennet:** trumpet.
  13.   **all-thing:** altogether.

59

Are with a most indissoluble tie
For ever knit.

Macbeth.

Ride you this afternoon?

Banquo.   Ay, my good lord.

Macbeth.

We should have else desired your good advice   20
(Which still° hath been both grave and prosperous)°
In this day's council; but we'll take tomorrow.
Is't far you ride?

Banquo.

As far, my lord, as will fill up the time
'Twixt this and supper. Go not my horse the better,°   25
I must become a borrower of the night
For a dark hour or twain.

Macbeth.   Fail not our feast.

Banquo.

My lord, I will not.

Macbeth.

We hear our bloody cousins are bestowed°
In England and in Ireland, not confessing   30
Their cruel parricide, filling their hearers
With strange invention.° But of that tomorrow,
When therewithal we shall have cause of state
Craving us jointly.° Hie you to horse. Adieu,
Till you return at night. Goes Fleance with you?   35

Banquo.

Ay, my good lord: our time does call upon's.

Macbeth.

I wish your horses swift and sure of foot,
And so I do commend you to their backs.
Farewell.   [*Exit* BANQUO.]

---

21. **still:** always. **grave and prosperous:** weighty and profitable.
25. **Go not my horse the better:** unless my horse goes faster than I expect.
29. **are bestowed:** have taken refuge.
32. **invention:** lies.
34. **us jointly:** our joint attention.

Let every man be master of his time   40
Till seven at night. To make society
The sweeter welcome, we will keep ourself
Till supper-time alone. While° then, God be with you!

Exeunt LORDS *and all but* MACBETH *and a* SERVANT.

Sirrah, a word with you: attend° those men
Our pleasure?   45
Attendant.
They are, my lord, without the palace gate.
Macbeth.
Bring them before us.   [*Exit* SERVANT.]
To be thus° is nothing, but° to be safely thus—
Our fears in Banquo stick deep,
And in his royalty of nature reigns that   50
Which would be feared. 'Tis much he dares;
And, to° that dauntless temper° of his mind,
He hath a wisdom that doth guide his valor
To act in safety. There is none but he
Whose being I do fear: and under him   55
My genius is rebuked,° as it is said
Mark Antony's was by Caesar. He chid the sisters,
When first they put the name of king upon me,
And bade them speak to him; then prophetlike
They hailed him father to a line of kings.   60
Upon my head they placed a fruitless crown
And put a barren scepter in my gripe,
Thence to be wrenched with an unlineal hand,
No son of mine succeeding. If't be so,
For Banquo's issue have I filed° my mind;   65
For them the gracious Duncan have I murdered;

---

43. **While:** until.
44. **attend:** await.
48. **thus:** king. **but:** unless.
52. **to:** added to. **temper:** quality.
56. **genius is rebuked:** guardian spirit is cowed.
65. **filed:** defiled; dirtied.

Put rancors° in the vessel of my peace
Only for them, and mine eternal jewel°
Given to the common enemy of man,°
To make them kings, the seeds of Banquo kings!   70
Rather than so, come, fate, into the list,°
And champion me to th' utterance!° Who's there?

Enter SERVANT *and two* MURDERERS.

Now go to the door, and stay there till we call.

                            Exit SERVANT.

Was it not yesterday we spoke together?
Murderers.
    It was, so please your highness.
Macbeth.   Well then, now   75
Have you considered of my speeches? Know
That it was he in the times past, which held you
So under fortune,° which you thought had been
Our innocent self: this I made good to you
In our last conference; passed in probation° with you,   80
How you were borne in hand,° how crossed; the
    instruments,°
Who wrought with them, and all things else that might
To half a soul° and to a notion° crazed
Say "Thus did Banquo."
First Murderer.   You made it known to us.
Macbeth.
I did so; and went further, which is now   85
Our point of second meeting. Do you find

---

67. **rancors:** bitter enmity.
68. **eternal jewel:** immortal soul.
69. **common enemy of man:** Satan.
71. **list:** battle.
72. **champion me to th' utterance:** fight against me till I give up.
78. **held you / So under fortune:** kept you from good fortune.
80. **probation:** review.
81. **borne in hand:** deceived. **instruments:** tools.
83. **soul:** brain. **notion:** mind.

Your patience so predominant in your nature,
That you can let this go? Are you so gospeled,°
To pray for this good man and for his issue,
Whose heavy hand hath bowed you to the grave   90
And beggared yours forever?

First Murderer.   We are men, my liege.

Macbeth.

Ay, in the catalogue ye go for° men;
As hounds and greyhounds, mongrels, spaniels, curs,
Shoughs, water-rugs° and demi-wolves, are clept°
All by the name of dogs: the valued file°   95
Distinguishes the swift, the slow, the subtle,
The housekeeper, the hunter, every one
According to the gift which bounteous nature
Hath in him closed,° whereby he does receive
Particular addition, from the bill°   100
That writes them all alike: and so of men.
Now if you have a station in the file,
Not i' th' worst rank of manhood, say't,
And I will put that business in your bosoms
Whose execution takes your enemy off,   105
Grapples you to the heart and love of us,
Who wear our health but sickly in his life,°
Which in his death were perfect.

Second Murderer.   I am one, my liege,
Whom the vile blows and buffets of the world
Hath so incensed that I am reckless what   110
I do to spite the world.

---

88. **gospeled:** so meek from reading the Gospel.
92. **go for:** pass as.
94. **Shoughs, water-rugs:** shaggy dogs and long-haired water dogs.
    clept: called.
95. **valued file:** classification by valuable traits.
99. **closed:** enclosed.
100. **bill:** list.
107. **Who wear . . . life:** who are "sick" while he (Banquo) still lives.

First Murderer.　　　　　And I another
　　So weary with disasters, tugged with fortune,
　　That I would set° my life on any chance,
　　To mend it or be rid on't.
Macbeth.　　　　　　　Both of you
　　Know Banquo was your enemy.
Both Murderers.　　　　　True, my lord.　　　　115
Macbeth.
　　So is he mine, and in such bloody distance°
　　That every minute of his being thrusts
　　Against my near'st of life:° and though I could
　　With barefaced power sweep him from my sight
　　And bid my will avouch° it, yet I must not,　　120
　　For° certain friends that are both his and mine,
　　Whose loves I may not drop, but wail his fall
　　Who I myself struck down: and thence it is
　　That I to your assistance do make love,
　　Masking the business from the common eye　　125
　　For sundry weighty reasons.
Second Murderer.　　　　　We shall, my lord,
　　Perform what you command us.
First Murderer.　　　　　Though our lives——
Macbeth.
　　Your spirits shine through you. Within this hour at
　　　　most
　　I will advise you where to plant yourselves,
　　Acquaint you with the perfect spy° o' th' time,　　130
　　The moment on't; for't must be done tonight,
　　And something° from the palace; always thought°
　　That I require a clearness:° and with him—

113.　**set:** risk.
116.　**distance:** quarrel.
118.　**near'st of life:** vital spot.
120.　**avouch:** justify.
121.　**For:** because of.
130.　**perfect spy:** exact information.
132.　**something:** some distance. **thought:** remembered.
133.　**clearness:** freedom from suspicion.

To leave no rubs° nor botches in the work—
Fleance his son, that keeps him company,   135
Whose absence is no less material to me
Than is his father's, must embrace the fate
Of that dark hour. Resolve yourselves apart:°
I'll come to you anon.
Murderers.   We are resolved, my lord.
Macbeth.
    I'll call upon you straight. Abide within.   140
    It is concluded: Banquo, thy soul's flight,
    If it find heaven, must find it out tonight.   [*Exeunt.*]

Scene 2. *The palace.*

Enter LADY MACBETH *and a* SERVANT.

Lady Macbeth.
    Is Banquo gone from court?
Servant.
    Ay, madam, but returns again tonight.
Lady Macbeth.
    Say to the king, I would attend his leisure
    For a few words.
Servant.   Madam, I will.   [*Exit.*]
Lady Macbeth.   Nought's had, all's spent,
    Where our desire is got without content: 5
    'Tis safer to be that which we destroy
    Than by destruction dwell in doubtful joy.

Enter MACBETH.

    How now, my lord! Why do you keep alone,
    Of sorriest fancies your companions making,
    Using those thoughts which should indeed have died   10

---

134. **rubs:** flaws.
138. **Resolve yourselves apart:** Make up your minds by yourselves.

With them they think on? Things without° all remedy
Should be without regard: what's done is done.

Macbeth.

We have scorched° the snake, not killed it:
She'll close° and be herself, whilst our poor malice°
Remains in danger of her former tooth.   15
But let the frame of things disjoint,° both the
    worlds° suffer,
Ere we will eat our meal in fear, and sleep
In the affliction of these terrible dreams
That shake us nightly: better be with the dead,
Whom we, to gain our peace, have sent to peace,   20
Than on the torture of the mind to lie
In restless ecstasy.° Duncan is in his grave;
After life's fitful fever he sleeps well.
Treason has done his worst: nor steel, nor poison,
Malice domestic,° foreign levy,° nothing,   25
Can touch him further.

Lady Macbeth.   Come on.

Gentle my lord, sleek° o'er your rugged° looks;
Be bright and jovial among your guests tonight.

Macbeth.

So shall I, love; and so, I pray, be you:
Let your remembrance apply to Banquo;°   30
Present him eminence,° both with eye and tongue:
Unsafe the while, that we must lave°
Our honors in these flattering streams

III.2.11. **without:** beyond.
  13. scorched: slashed.
  14. close: heal. **malice:** enmity; hatred.
  16. frame of things disjoint: universe collapse. **worlds:** heaven and earth.
  22. ecstasy: frenzy.
  25. Malice domestic: domestic war (civil war). **foreign levy:** exaction of
      tribute by a foreign country.
  27. sleek: smooth. **rugged:** furrowed.
  30. Let . . . Banquo: That is, focus your thoughts on Banquo.
  31. eminence: honors.
  32. lave: wash.

And make our faces vizards° to our hearts,
Disguising what they are.
Lady Macbeth.   You must leave this.   35
Macbeth.

O, full of scorpions is my mind, dear wife!
Thou know'st that Banquo, and his Fleance, lives.
Lady Macbeth.

But in them nature's copy's not eterne.°
Macbeth.

There's comfort yet; they are assailable.
Then be thou jocund. Ere the bat hath flown   40
His cloistered flight, ere to black Hecate's summons
The shard-borne° beetle with his drowsy hums
Hath rung night's yawning peal, there shall be done
A deed of dreadful note.
Lady Macbeth.   What's to be done?
Macbeth.

Be innocent of the knowledge, dearest chuck,°   45
Till thou applaud the deed. Come, seeling° night,
Scarf up° the tender eye of pitiful day,
And with thy bloody and invisible hand
Cancel and tear to pieces that great bond
Which keeps me pale! Light thickens, and the crow   50
Makes wing to th' rooky° wood.
Good things of day begin to droop and drowse,
Whiles night's black agents to their preys do rouse.
Thou marvel'st at my words: but hold thee still;
Things bad begun make strong themselves by ill: 55
So, prithee, go with me.   [*Exeunt.*]

---

34. **vizards:** masks.
38. **nature's copy's not eterne:** That is, they won't live forever.
42. **shard-borne:** carried on scaly wings.
45. **chuck:** chick (a term of endearment).
46. **seeling:** eye-closing; blinding.
47. **Scarf up:** blindfold.
51. **rooky:** full of rooks, or crows.

Scene 3. *Near the palace.*

Enter three MURDERERS.

First Murderer.
    But who did bid thee join with us?
Third Murderer.   Macbeth.
Second Murderer.
    He needs not our mistrust; since he delivers
    Our offices and what we have to do
    To the direction just.°
First Murderer.   Then stand with us.
    The west yet glimmers with some streaks of day.   5
    Now spurs the lated° traveler apace
    To gain the timely inn, and near approaches
    The subject of our watch.
Third Murderer.   Hark! I hear horses.
Banquo (*within*).
    Give us a light there, ho!
Second Murderer.   Then 'tis he. The rest
    That are within the note of expectation°   10
    Already are i' th' court.
First Murderer.   His horses go about.
Third Murderer.
    Almost a mile: but he does usually—
    So all men do—from hence to th' palace gate
    Make it their walk.

Enter BANQUO *and* FLEANCE, *with a torch.*

Second Murderer.
    A light, a light!
Third Murderer.   'Tis he.
First Murderer.   Stand to't.   15

III.3.4. **He needs . . . just:** We need not mistrust him (the Third Murderer)
    since he describes our duties exactly according to our directions.
  6. **lated:** belated.
 10. **within . . . expectation:** on the list of expected guests.

Banquo.

It will be rain tonight.

First Murderer.   Let it come down.

They set upon BANQUO.

Banquo.

O, treachery! Fly, good Fleance, fly, fly, fly!

Exit FLEANCE.

Thou mayst revenge. O slave!   [*Dies.*]

Third Murderer.

Who did strike out the light?

First Murderer.   Was't not the way?°

Third Murderer.

There's but one down; the son is fled.   20

Second Murderer.

We have lost best half of our affair.

First Murderer.

Well, let's away and say how much is done. [*Exeunt.*]

Scene 4. *The palace.*

Banquet prepared. Enter MACBETH, LADY MACBETH, ROSS,
LENNOX, LORDS, *and* ATTENDANTS.

Macbeth.

You know your own degrees;° sit down:

At first and last, the hearty welcome.

Lords.

Thanks to your majesty.

Macbeth.

Oneself will mingle with society°

And play the humble host.   5

---

19. **way:** thing to do.

III.4.1. **degrees:** ranks.

4. **society:** the company.

Our hostess keeps her state,° but in best time
We will require° her welcome.
Lady Macbeth.
Pronounce it for me, sir, to all our friends,
For my heart speaks they are welcome.

Enter FIRST MURDERER.

Macbeth.
See, they encounter° thee with their hearts' thanks.   10
Both sides are even: here I'll sit i' th' midst:
Be large in mirth; anon we'll drink a measure°
The table round. (*Goes to* FIRST MURDERER.) There's
     blood upon thy face.
Murderer.
'Tis Banquo's then.
Macbeth.
'Tis better thee without than he within.°   15
Is he dispatched?
Murderer.   My lord, his throat is cut;
That I did for him.
Macbeth.   Thou art the best o' th' cutthroats.
Yet he's good that did the like for Fleance;
If thou didst it, thou art the nonpareil.
Murderer.
Most royal sir, Fleance is 'scaped.   20
Macbeth (*aside*).
Then comes my fit again: I had else been perfect,
Whole as the marble, founded° as the rock,
As broad and general as the casing air:°

---

6. **keeps her state:** remains seated in her chair of state.
7. **require:** request.
10. **encounter:** meet.
12. **measure:** goblet.
15. **thee . . . within:** outside you than inside him.
22. **founded:** firmly based.
23. **broad . . . casing air:** unconfined as the surrounding air.

But now I am cabined, cribbed,° confined, bound in
To saucy° doubts and fears.—But Banquo's safe?   25
Murderer.
Ay, my good lord: safe in a ditch he bides,
With twenty trenchèd° gashes on his head,
The least a death to nature.
Macbeth.   Thanks for that.
(*Aside.*) There the grown serpent lies; the worm°
     that's fled
Hath nature that in time will venom breed,   30
No teeth for th' present. Get thee gone. Tomorrow
We'll hear ourselves° again.   [*Exit* FIRST MURDERER.]
Lady Macbeth.   My royal lord,
You do not give the cheer.° The feast is sold
That is not often vouched, while 'tis a-making,
'Tis given with welcome. To feed were best at home;°   35
From thence, the sauce to meat° is ceremony;
Meeting were bare without it.

Enter the GHOST OF BANQUO, *and sits in Macbeth's place.*

Macbeth.   Sweet remembrancer!°
Now good digestion wait on appetite,
And health on both!
Lennox.   May't please your highness sit.
Macbeth.
Here had we now our country's honor roofed,°   40
Were the graced person of our Banquo present—

---

24. **cribbed:** penned up.
25. **saucy:** insolent.
27. **trenchèd:** trenchlike.
29. **worm:** serpent.
32. **hear ourselves:** talk it over.
33. **cheer:** sense of cordiality.
35. **The feast . . . home:** The feast seems sold (not given) when the host
     fails to welcome the guests. Mere eating is best done at home.
36. **meat:** food.
37. **remembrancer:** reminder.
40. **our . . . roofed:** our nobility under one roof.

Who may I rather challenge for unkindness
Than pity for mischance!°

Ross.   His absence, sir,
Lays blame upon his promise. Please't your highness
To grace us with your royal company?   45

Macbeth.
The table's full.

Lennox.   Here is a place reserved, sir.

Macbeth.
Where?

Lennox.
Here, my good lord. What is't that moves your
    highness?

Macbeth.
Which of you have done this?

Lords.   What, my good lord?

Macbeth.
Thou canst not say I did it. Never shake   50
Thy gory locks at me.

Ross.
Gentlemen, rise, his highness is not well.

Lady Macbeth.
Sit, worthy friends. My Lord is often thus,
And hath been from his youth. Pray you, keep seat.
The fit is momentary; upon a thought°   55
He will again be well. If much you note him,
You shall offend him and extend his passion.°
Feed, and regard him not.—Are you a man?

Macbeth.
Ay, and a bold one, that dare look on that
Which might appall the devil.

---

43. **Who . . . mischance:** whom I hope I may reprove because he is
    unkind rather than pity because he has encountered an accident.
55. **upon a thought:** as quick as a thought.
57. **extend his passion:** lengthen his fit.

Lady Macbeth.   O proper stuff!   60
  This is the very painting of your fear.
  This is the air-drawn dagger which, you said,
  Led you to Duncan. O, these flaws° and starts,
  Imposters to° true fear, would well become
  A woman's story at a winter's fire,   65
  Authorized° by her grandam. Shame itself!
  Why do you make such faces? When all's done,
  You look but on a stool.
Macbeth.   Prithee, see there!
  Behold! Look! Lo! How say you?
  Why, what care I? If thou canst nod, speak too.   70
  If charnel houses° and our graves must send
  Those that we bury back, our monuments
  Shall be the maws of kites.°   [*Exit* GHOST.]
Lady Macbeth.   What, quite unmanned in folly?
Macbeth.
  If I stand here, I saw him.
Lady Macbeth.   Fie, for shame!
Macbeth.
  Blood hath been shed ere now, i' th' olden time,   75
  Ere humane statute purged the gentle weal;°
  Ay, and since too, murders have been performed
  Too terrible for the ear. The time has been
  That, when the brains were out, the man would die,
  And there an end; but now they rise again,   80
  With twenty mortal murders on their crowns,°
  And push us from our stools. This is more strange
  Than such a murder is.

---

63. **flaws:** gusts; outbursts.
64. **to:** compared with.
66. **Authorized:** vouched for.
71. **charnel houses:** vaults containing bones.
73. **our . . . kites:** Our tombs shall be the bellies of rapacious birds.
76. **purged . . . weal:** cleansed the state and made it gentle.
81. **mortal . . . crowns:** deadly wounds on their heads.

Lady Macbeth.   My worthy lord,
  Your noble friends do lack you.
Macbeth.   I do forget.
  Do not muse at me, my most worthy friends;   85
  I have a strange infirmity, which is nothing
  To those that know me. Come, love and health to all!
  Then I'll sit down. Give me some wine, fill full.

Enter GHOST.

  I drink to th' general joy o' th' whole table,
  And to our dear friend Banquo, whom we miss;   90
  Would he were here! To all and him we thirst,°
  And all to all.°
Lords.   Our duties, and the pledge.
Macbeth.
  Avaunt! and quit my sight! Let the earth hide thee!
  Thy bones are marrowless, thy blood is cold;
  Thou hast no speculation° in those eyes   95
  Which thou dost glare with.
Lady Macbeth.   Think of this, good peers,
  But as a thing of custom; 'tis no other.
  Only it spoils the pleasure of the time.
Macbeth.
  What man dare, I dare.
  Approach thou like the rugged Russian bear,   100
  The armed rhinoceros, or th' Hyrcan° tiger;
  Take any shape but that, and my firm nerves°
  Shall never tremble. Or be alive again,
  And dare me to the desert° with thy sword.
  If trembling I inhabit then, protest me   105

---

91. **thirst:** desire to drink.
92. **all to all:** Let everybody drink to everybody.
95. **speculation:** sight.
101. **Hyrcan:** of Hyrcania (near the Caspian Sea).
102. **nerves:** sinews.
104. **desert:** lonely place.

The baby of a girl.° Hence, horrible shadow!
Unreal mock'ry, hence!   [*Exit* GHOST.]
                    Why, so: being gone,
I am a man again. Pray you, sit still.
Lady Macbeth.
    You have displaced the mirth, broke the good meeting,
    With most admired° disorder.
Macbeth.   Can such things be,   110
    And overcome us° like a summer's cloud,
    Without our special wonder? You make me strange
    Even to the disposition that I owe,°
    When now I think you can behold such sights,
    And keep the natural ruby of your cheeks,   115
    When mine is blanched with fear.
Ross.   What sights, my lord?
Lady Macbeth.
    I pray you, speak not: he grows worse and worse;
    Question enrages him: at once, good night.
    Stand not upon the order of your going,°
    But go at once.
Lennox.   Good night; and better health   120
    Attend his majesty!
Lady Macbeth.   A kind good night to all!

                    Exeunt LORDS.

Macbeth.
    It will have blood, they say: blood will have blood.
    Stones have been known to move and trees to speak;
    Augurs and understood relations° have

---

106. **If . . . girl:** If I tremble then, proclaim me a baby girl.
110. **admired:** amazing.
111. **overcome us:** come over us.
113. **You . . . owe:** You make me wonder what my nature is.
119. **Stand . . . going:** Do not insist on departing in your order of rank.
124. **Augurs . . . relations:** auguries (omens) and comprehended reports.

By maggot-pies and choughs and rooks brought forth°   125
The secret'st man of blood. What is the night?°
Lady Macbeth.
    Almost at odds with morning, which is which.
Macbeth.
    How say'st thou, that Macduff denies his person
    At our great bidding?
Lady Macbeth.   Did you send to him, sir?
Macbeth.
    I hear it by the way,° but I will send: 130
    There's not a one of them but in his house
    I keep a servant fee'd.° I will tomorrow,
    And betimes° I will, to the weird sisters:
    More shall they speak, for now I am bent° to know
    By the worst means the worst. For mine own good   135
    All causes° shall give way. I am in blood
    Stepped in so far that, should I wade no more,
    Returning were as tedious as go o'er.
    Strange things I have in head that will to hand,
    Which must be acted ere they may be scanned.°   140
Lady Macbeth.
    You lack the season of all natures,° sleep.
Macbeth.
    Come, we'll to sleep. My strange and self-abuse°
    Is the initiate fear that wants hard use.°
    We are yet but young in deed.   [*Exeunt.*]

---

125. **By . . . forth:** by magpies, crows, and rooks (telltale birds) revealed.
126. **What . . . night:** What time of night is it?
130. **by the way:** incidentally.
132. **fee'd:** that is, paid to spy.
133. **betimes:** quickly.
134. **bent:** determined.
136. **causes:** considerations.
140. **may be scanned:** can be examined.
141. **season . . . natures:** seasoning (preservative) of all living creatures.
142. **self-abuse:** delusion.
143. **initiate . . . use:** beginner's fear that lacks hardening practice.

Scene 5. *A witches' haunt.*

Thunder. Enter the three WITCHES, *meeting* HECATE.

First Witch.
    Why, how now, Hecate! you look angerly.
Hecate.
    Have I not reason, beldams° as you are,
    Saucy and overbold? How did you dare
    To trade and traffic with Macbeth
    In riddles and affairs of death;   5
    And I, the mistress of your charms,
    The close contriver° of all harms,
    Was never called to bear my part,
    Or show the glory of our art?
    And, which is worse, all you have done   10
    Hath been but for a wayward son,
    Spiteful and wrathful; who, as others do,
    Loves for his own ends, not for you.
    But make amends now: get you gone,
    And at the pit of Acheron°   15
    Meet me i' th' morning: thither he
    Will come to know his destiny.
    Your vessels and your spells provide,
    Your charms and everything beside.
    I am for th' air; this night I'll spend   20
    Unto a dismal and a fatal end:
    Great business must be wrought ere noon.
    Upon the corner of the moon
    There hangs a vap'rous drop profound;°
    I'll catch it ere it come to ground: 25
    And that distilled by magic sleights°

III.5.2. **beldams:** hags.
   7. **close contriver:** secret inventor.
  15. **Acheron:** river of Hades.
  24. **profound:** heavy.
  26. **sleights:** arts.

Shall raise such artificial sprites°
As by the strength of their illusion
Shall draw him on to his confusion.°
He shall spurn fate, scorn death, and bear   30
His hopes 'bove wisdom, grace, and fear:
And you all know security°
Is mortal's chiefest enemy.

Music and a song.

Hark! I am called; my little spirit, see,
Sits in a foggy cloud and stays for me.   [*Exit.*]   35

Sing within, "Come away, come away," *etc.*

First Witch.
Come, let's make haste; she'll soon be back again.

Exeunt.

Scene 6. *The palace.*

Enter LENNOX *and another* LORD.

Lennox.
My former speeches have but hit your thoughts,°
Which can interpret farther. Only I say
Things have been strangely borne.° The gracious
Duncan
Was pitied of Macbeth: marry, he was dead.
And the right-valiant Banquo walked too late;   5
Whom, you may say, if't please you, Fleance killed,
For Fleance fled. Men must not walk too late.

---

27. **artificial sprites:** spirits created by magic arts.
29. **confusion:** ruin.
32. **security:** overconfidence.
III.6.1. **My . . . thoughts:** My recent words have only coincided with what
        you have in your mind.
  3. **borne:** managed.

Who cannot want the thought,° how monstrous
It was for Malcolm and for Donalbain
To kill their gracious father? Damnèd fact!°   10
How it did grieve Macbeth! Did he not straight,
In pious rage, the two delinquents tear,
That were the slaves of drink and thralls° of sleep?
Was not that nobly done? Ay, and wisely too;
For 'twould have angered any heart alive   15
To hear the men deny't. So that I say
He has borne all things well: and I do think
That, had he Duncan's sons under his key—
As, an't° please heaven, he shall not—they should find
What 'twere to kill a father. So should Fleance.   20
But, peace! for from broad words,° and 'cause he failed
His presence at the tyrant's feast, I hear,
Macduff lives in disgrace. Sir, can you tell
Where he bestows himself?

Lord.   The son of Duncan,
From whom this tyrant holds the due of birth,°   25
Lives in the English court, and is received
Of the most pious Edward° with such grace
That the malevolence of fortune nothing
Takes from his high respect.° Thither Macduff
Is gone to pray the holy king, upon his aid°   30
To wake Northumberland° and warlike Siward;°
That by the help of these, with Him above

---

8. **cannot . . . thought:** cannot help but think.
10. **fact:** evil deed.
13. **thralls:** slaves.
19. **an't:** if it.
21. **for . . . words:** because of frank talk.
25. **due of birth:** birthright.
27. **Edward:** Edward the Confessor (reigned 1042–1066).
29. **nothing . . . respect:** does not diminish the high respect in which he is held.
30. **upon his aid:** to aid him (Malcolm).
31. **To wake Northumberland:** that is, to arouse the people in an English county near Scotland. **Siward:** earl of Northumberland.

To ratify the work, we may again
Give to our tables meat, sleep to our nights,
Free from our feasts and banquets bloody knives,   35
Do faithful homage and receive free° honors:
All which we pine for now. And this report
Hath so exasperate the king that he
Prepares for some attempt of war.

Lennox.   Sent he to Macduff?

Lord.

He did: and with an absolute "Sir, not I,"   40
The cloudy° messenger turns me his back,
And hums, as who should say "You'll rue the time
That clogs° me with this answer."

Lennox.   And that well might
Advise him to a caution, t' hold what distance
His wisdom can provide. Some holy angel   45
Fly to the court of England and unfold
His message ere he come, that a swift blessing
May soon return to this our suffering country
Under a hand accursed!

Lord.   I'll send my prayers with him.

Exeunt.

---

36. free: freely granted.
41. cloudy: disturbed.
43. clogs: burdens.

Act IV

Scene 1. *A witches' haunt.*

Thunder. Enter the three WITCHES.

First Witch.
　Thrice the brinded° cat hath mewed.
Second Witch.
　Thrice and once the hedge-pig° whined.
Third Witch.
　Harpier° cries, 'Tis time, 'tis time.
First Witch.
　Round about the caldron go:
　In the poisoned entrails throw.　　　　　　　　　5
　Toad, that under cold stone
　Days and nights has thirty-one
　Swelt'red venom sleeping got,°
　Boil thou first i' th' charmèd pot.
All.
　Double, double, toil and trouble;　　　　　　　10
　Fire burn and caldron bubble.
Second Witch.
　Fillet° of a fenny° snake,
　In the caldron boil and bake;
　Eye of newt and toe of frog,
　Wool of bat and tongue of dog,　　　　　　　15

IV.1.1.　**brinded:** brindled.
　2.　**hedge-pig:** hedgehog.
　3.　**Harpier:** an attendant spirit, like Graymalkin and Paddock in Act I,
　　　Scene 1.
　8.　**Swelt'red . . . got:** venom sweated out during sleep.
　12.　**Fillet:** slice. **fenny:** from a swamp.

Adder's fork° and blindworm's° sting,
Lizard's leg and howlet's° wing,
For a charm of pow'rful trouble,
Like a hell-broth boil and bubble.
All.
Double, double, toil and trouble;   20
Fire burn and caldron bubble.
Third Witch.
Scale of dragon, tooth of wolf,
Witch's mummy,° maw and gulf°
Of the ravined° salt-sea shark,
Root of hemlock digged i' th' dark,   25
Liver of blaspheming Jew,
Gall of goat, and slips of yew
Slivered in the moon's eclipse,
Nose of Turk and Tartar's lips,
Finger of birth-strangled babe   30
Ditch-delivered by a drab,°
Make the gruel thick and slab:°
Add thereto a tiger's chaudron,°
For th' ingredients of our caldron.
All.
Double, double, toil and trouble;   35
Fire burn and caldron bubble.
Second Witch.
Cool it with a baboon's blood,
Then the charm is firm and good.

Enter HECATE *and the other three* WITCHES.

---

16. **fork:** forked tongue. **blindworm's:** legless lizard's.
17. **howlet's:** owl's.
23. **Witch's mummy:** mummified flesh of a witch. **maw and gulf:** stomach and gullet.
24. **ravined:** ravenous.
31. **drab:** harlot.
32. **slab:** slimy.
33. **chaudron:** entrails.

Hecate.

> O, well done! I commend your pains;
> And every one shall share i' th' gains: 40
> And now about the caldron sing,
> Like elves and fairies in a ring,
> Enchanting all that you put in.

Music and a song: "Black Spirits," *etc.*

> *Exeunt* HECATE *and the other three* WITCHES.

Second Witch.

> By the pricking of my thumbs,
> Something wicked this way comes: 45
>> Open, locks,
>> Whoever knocks!

Enter MACBETH.

Macbeth.

> How now, you secret, black, and midnight hags!
> What is't you do?
>
All.   A deed without a name.

Macbeth.

> I conjure you, by that which you profess,   50
> Howe'er you come to know it, answer me:
> Though you untie the winds and let them fight
> Against the churches; though the yesty° waves
> Confound° and swallow navigation up;
> Though bladed corn be lodged° and trees blown down;   55
> Though castles topple on their warders' heads;
> Though palaces and pyramids do slope°
> Their heads to their foundations; though the treasure
> Of nature's germens° tumble all together,

---

53. **yesty:** foamy.
54. **Confound:** destroy.
55. **bladed . . . lodged:** grain in the ear be beaten down.
57. **slope:** bend.
59. **nature's germens:** seeds of all life.

Even till destruction sicken,° answer me   60
To what I ask you.
First Witch.   Speak.
Second Witch.   Demand.
Third Witch.   We'll answer.
First Witch.
    Say, if th' hadst rather hear it from our mouths,
    Or from our masters?
Macbeth.   Call 'em, let me see 'em.
First Witch.
    Pour in sow's blood, that hath eaten
    Her nine farrow;° grease that's sweaten°   65
    From the murderer's gibbet° throw
    Into the flame.
All.   Come, high or low,
    Thyself and office° deftly show!

Thunder. FIRST APPARITION: *an Armed Head.*°

Macbeth.
    Tell me, thou unknown power——
First Witch.   He knows thy thought:
    Hear his speech, but say thou nought.   70
First Apparition.
    Macbeth! Macbeth! Macbeth! Beware Macduff!
    Beware the Thane of Fife. Dismiss me: enough.

                        He descends.

Macbeth.
    Whate'er thou art, for thy good caution thanks:
    Thou hast harped° my fear aright. But one word
        more——

---

60. **sicken:** sicken at its own work.
65. **farrow:** young pigs. **sweaten:** sweated.
66. **gibbet:** gallows.
68. **office:** function.
s.d. **Armed Head:** helmeted head.
74. **harped:** hit upon; struck the note of.

First Witch.

>He will not be commanded. Here's another, 75
>
>More potent than the first.

Thunder. SECOND APPARITION: *a Bloody Child.*

Second Apparition.

>Macbeth! Macbeth! Macbeth!

Macbeth.

>Had I three ears, I'd hear thee.

Second Apparition.

>Be bloody, bold, and resolute! Laugh to scorn
>
>The pow'r of man, for none of woman born 80
>
>Shall harm Macbeth. [*Descends.*]

Macbeth.

>Then live, Macduff: what need I fear of thee?
>
>But yet I'll make assurance double sure,
>
>And take a bond of fate.° Thou shalt not live;
>
>That I may tell pale-hearted fear it lies, 85
>
>And sleep in spite of thunder.

Thunder. THIRD APPARITION: *a Child Crowned, with a tree in his hand.*

>What is this,
>
>That rises like the issue° of a king,
>
>And wears upon his baby-brow the round
>
>And top of sovereignty?°

All. Listen, but speak not to't.

Third Apparition.

>Be lion-mettled, proud, and take no care 90
>
>Who chafes, who frets, or where conspirers are:
>
>Macbeth shall never vanquished be until
>
>Great Birnam Wood to high Dunsinane Hill
>
>Shall come against him. [*Descends.*]

---

84. **take . . . fate:** get a guarantee from fate (that is, he will kill Macduff and thus will compel fate to keep its word).

87. **issue:** offspring.

89. **round . . . sovereignty:** that is, crown.

Macbeth.   That will never be.
Who can impress° the forest, bid the tree   95
Unfix his earth-bound root? Sweet bodements,° good!
Rebellious dead, rise never, till the Wood
Of Birnam rise, and our high-placed Macbeth
Shall live the lease of nature,° pay his breath
To time and mortal custom.° Yet my heart   100
Throbs to know one thing. Tell me, if your art
Can tell so much: shall Banquo's issue ever
Reign in this kingdom?
All.   Seek to know no more.
Macbeth.
I will be satisfied.° Deny me this,
And an eternal curse fall on you! Let me know.   105
Why sinks that caldron? And what noise° is this?

Hautboys.

First Witch. Show!
Second Witch. Show!
Third Witch. Show!
All.
Show his eyes, and grieve his heart;   110
Come like shadows, so depart!

A show of eight KINGS *and* BANQUO, *last* KING *with a glass in his hand.*

Macbeth.
Thou art too like the spirit of Banquo. Down!
Thy crown does sear mine eyelids. And thy hair,
Thou other gold-bound brow, is like the first.
A third is like the former. Filthy hags!   115

---

95. **impress:** conscript; draft.
96. **bodements:** prophecies.
99. **lease of nature:** natural life span.
100. **mortal custom:** natural death.
104. **satisfied:** that is, fully informed.
106. **noise:** music.

Why do you show me this? A fourth! Start,° eyes!
What, will the line stretch out to th' crack of doom?°
Another yet! A seventh! I'll see no more.
And yet the eighth° appears, who bears a glass
Which shows me many more; and some I see   120
That twofold balls and treble scepters° carry:
Horrible sight! Now I see 'tis true;
For the blood-boltered° Banquo smiles upon me,
And points at them for his.° What, is this so?

First Witch.

Ay, sir, all this is so. But why   125
Stands Macbeth thus amazedly?
Come, sisters, cheer we up his sprites,°
And show the best of our delights:
I'll charm the air to give a sound,
While you perform your antic round,°   130
That this great king may kindly say
Our duties did his welcome pay.

Music. The WITCHES *dance, and vanish.*

Macbeth.

Where are they? Gone? Let this pernicious hour
Stand aye accursèd in the calendar!
Come in, without there!

Enter LENNOX.

Lennox.   What's your grace's will?   135

Macbeth.

Saw you the weird sisters?

---

116. **Start:** that is, from the sockets.
117. **crack of doom:** blast (of a trumpet) on doomsday.
119. **eighth:** James I of England, who was the king at the time the play
     was written.
121. **twofold . . . scepters:** coronation emblems.
123. **blood-boltered:** matted with blood.
124. **his:** his descendants.
127. **sprites:** spirits.
130. **antic round:** grotesque circular dance.

Lennox.   No, my lord.
Macbeth.
  Came they not by you?
Lennox.   No indeed, my lord.
Macbeth.
  Infected by the air whereon they ride,
  And damned all those that trust them! I did hear
  The galloping of horse.° Who was't came by?   140
Lennox.
  'Tis two or three, my lord, that bring you word
  Macduff is fled to England.
Macbeth.   Fled to England?
Lennox.
  Ay, my good lord.
Macbeth (*aside*).
  Time, thou anticipat'st° my dread exploits.
  The flighty purpose never is o'ertook   145
  Unless the deed go with it.° From this moment
  The very firstlings of my heart° shall be
  The firstlings of my hand. And even now,
  To crown my thoughts with acts, be it thought and
      done:
  The castle of Macduff I will surprise;°   150
  Seize upon Fife; give to th' edge o' th' sword
  His wife, his babes, and all unfortunate souls
  That trace him in his line.° No boasting like a fool;
  This deed I'll do before this purpose cool:
  But no more sights!—Where are these gentlemen?   155
  Come, bring me where they are.   [*Exeunt.*]

---

140. **horse:** horses (or horsemen).
144. **anticipat'st:** foretold.
146. **The flighty . . . it:** The fleeting plan is never accomplished unless an
     action accompanies it.
147. **firstlings . . . heart:** first thoughts; impulses.
150. **surprise:** attack suddenly.
153. **trace . . . line:** are of his lineage.

Scene 2. *Macduff's castle.*

Enter Macduff's wife LADY MACDUFF, *her* SON, *and* ROSS.

Lady Macduff.
 What had he done, to make him fly the land?
Ross.
 You must have patience, madam.
Lady Macduff.   He had none:
 His flight was madness. When our actions do not,
 Our fears do make us traitors.
Ross.   You know not
 Whether it was his wisdom or his fear.   5
Lady Macduff.
 Wisdom! To leave his wife, to leave his babes,
 His mansion and his titles,° in a place
 From whence himself does fly? He loves us not;
 He wants the natural touch:° for the poor wren,
 The most diminutive of birds, will fight,   10
 Her young ones in her nest, against the owl.
 All is the fear and nothing is the love;
 As little is the wisdom, where the flight
 So runs against all reason.
Ross.   My dearest coz,°
 I pray you, school° yourself. But, for your husband,   15
 He is noble, wise, judicious, and best knows
 The fits o' th' season.° I dare not speak much further:
 But cruel are the times, when we are traitors
 And do not know ourselves; when we hold rumor
 From what we fear,° yet know not what we fear,   20

IV.2.7. **titles:** possessions.
 9. **wants . . . touch:** that is, lacks natural affection for his wife and
   children.
 14. **coz:** cousin.
 15. **school:** control.
 17. **fits . . . season:** disorders of the time.
 20. **hold . . . fear:** believe rumors because we fear.

But float upon a wild and violent sea
Each way and move. I take my leave of you.
Shall not be long but I'll be here again.
Things at the worst will cease,° or else climb upward
To what they were before. My pretty cousin,   25
Blessing upon you!
Lady Macduff.
Fathered he is, and yet he's fatherless.
Ross.
I am so much a fool, should I stay longer,
It would be my disgrace° and your discomfort.
I take my leave at once.   [*Exit* ROSS.]
Lady Macduff.   Sirrah,° your father's dead: 30
And what will you do now? How will you live?
Son.
As birds do, mother.
Lady Macduff.   What, with worms and flies?
Son.
With what I get, I mean; and so do they.
Lady Macduff.
Poor bird! thou'dst never fear the net nor lime,°
The pitfall nor the gin.°   35
Son.
Why should I, mother? Poor birds they are not
    set for.
My father is not dead, for all your saying.
Lady Macduff.
Yes, he is dead: how wilt thou do for a father?
Son. Nay, how will you do for a husband?
Lady Macduff. Why, I can buy me twenty at any market.   40
Son. Then you'll buy 'em to sell° again.

---

24. **cease:** cease worsening.
29. **It . . . disgrace:** That is, I would weep.
30. **Sirrah:** here, an affectionate form of address to a child.
34. **lime:** birdlime (smeared on branches to catch birds).
35. **gin:** trap.
41. **sell:** betray.

Lady Macduff.
Thou speak'st with all thy wit, and yet, i' faith,
With wit enough for thee.°

Son.
Was my father a traitor, mother?

Lady Macduff. Ay, that he was.   45

Son. What is a traitor?

Lady Macduff. Why, one that swears and lies.°

Son. And be all traitors that do so?

Lady Macduff. Every one that does so is a traitor, and
   must be hanged.   50

Son. And must they all be hanged that swear and lie?

Lady Macduff. Every one.

Son. Who must hang them?

Lady Macduff. Why, the honest men.

Son. Then the liars and swearers are fools; for there are   55
   liars and swearers enow° to beat the honest men
   and hang up them.

Lady Macduff. Now, God help thee, poor monkey! But
   how wilt thou do for a father?

Son. If he were dead, you'd weep for him. If you would   60
   not, it were a good sign that I should quickly have a
   new father.

Lady Macduff. Poor prattler, how thou talk'st!

Enter a MESSENGER.

Messenger.
Bless you, fair dame! I am not to you known,
Though in your state of honor I am perfect.°   65
I doubt° some danger does approach you nearly:
If you will take a homely° man's advice,

---

43. **for thee:** for a child.
47. **swears and lies:** takes an oath and breaks it.
56. **enow:** enough.
65. **in . . . perfect:** That is, I am fully informed of your honorable rank.
66. **doubt:** fear.
67. **homely:** plain.

Be not found here; hence, with your little ones.
To fright you thus, methinks I am too savage;
To do worse to you were fell° cruelty,   70
Which is too nigh your person. Heaven preserve
     you!
I dare abide no longer.   [*Exit* MESSENGER.]
Lady Macduff.   Whither should I fly?
I have done no harm. But I remember now
I am in this earthly world, where to do harm
Is often laudable, to do good sometime   75
Accounted dangerous folly. Why then, alas,
Do I put up that womanly defense,
To say I have done no harm?—What are these
     faces?

Enter MURDERERS.

Murderer.
Where is your husband?
Lady Macduff.
I hope, in no place so unsanctified   80
Where such as thou mayst find him.
Murderer.   He's a traitor.
Son.
Thou li'st, thou shag-eared° villain!
Murderer.   What, you egg!

Stabbing him.

Young fry° of treachery!
Son.   He has killed me, mother:
Run away, I pray you!   [*Dies.*]

          Exit LADY MACDUFF, *crying* "Murder!" *followed by*
                                        MURDERERS.

---

70. **fell:** fierce.
82. **shag-eared:** hairy-eared.
83. **fry:** spawn.

Scene 3. *England. Before the king's palace.*

Enter MALCOLM *and* MACDUFF.

Malcolm.
Let us seek out some desolate shade, and there
Weep our sad bosoms empty.
Macduff.   Let us rather
Hold fast the mortal° sword, and like good men
Bestride our down-fall'n birthdom.° Each new
    morn
New widows howl, new orphans cry, new sorrows   5
Strike heaven on the face, that° it resounds
As if it felt with Scotland and yelled out
Like syllable of dolor.°
Malcolm.   What I believe, I'll wail;
What know, believe; and what I can redress,
As I shall find the time to friend,° I will.   10
What you have spoke, it may be so perchance.
This tyrant, whose sole° name blisters our tongues,
Was once thought honest:° you have loved him
    well;
He hath not touched you yet. I am young; but
    something
You may deserve of him through me;° and wisdom°   15
To offer up a weak, poor, innocent lamb
T' appease an angry god.
Macduff.
I am not treacherous.

IV.3.3. **mortal:** deadly.
  4. **Bestride . . . birthdom:** protectively stand over our native land.
  6. **that:** so that.
  8. **Like . . . dolor:** similar sound of grief.
 10. **to friend:** to be friendly or favorable.
 12. **sole:** very.
 13. **honest:** good.
 15. **deserve . . . me:** that is, earn by betraying me to Macbeth. **wisdom:** it
      may be wise.

Malcolm.   But Macbeth is.
   A good and virtuous nature may recoil
   In° an imperial charge. But I shall crave your pardon;   20
   That which you are, my thoughts cannot transpose:°
   Angels are bright still, though the brightest° fell:
   Though all things foul would wear° the brows of
      grace,
   Yet grace must still look so.°

Macduff.   I have lost my hopes.

Malcolm.
   Perchance even there where I did find my doubts.   25
   Why in that rawness° left you wife and child,
   Those precious motives, those strong knots of love,
   Without leave-taking? I pray you,
   Let not my jealousies° be your dishonors,
   But mine own safeties. You may be rightly just°   30
   Whatever I shall think.

Macduff.   Bleed, bleed, poor country:
   Great tyranny, lay thou thy basis° sure,
   For goodness dare not check° thee: wear thou thy
      wrongs;
   The title is affeered.° Fare thee well, lord:
   I would not be the villain that thou think'st   35
   For the whole space that's in the tyrant's grasp
   And the rich East to boot.

---

20. **recoil / In:** give way under.
21. **transpose:** transform.
22. **the brightest:** Lucifer, the angel who led the revolt of the angels and
    was thrown out of heaven; Satan.
23. **would wear:** desire to wear.
24. **so:** like itself.
26. **rawness:** unprotected condition.
29. **jealousies:** suspicions.
30. **rightly just:** perfectly honorable.
32. **basis:** foundation.
33. **check:** restrain.
34. **affeered:** legally confirmed.

Malcolm.   Be not offended:
I speak not as in absolute fear of you.
I think our country sinks beneath the yoke;
It weeps, it bleeds, and each new day a gash   40
Is added to her wounds. I think withal°
There would be hands uplifted in my right;°
And here from gracious England° have I offer
Of goodly thousands: but, for° all this,
When I shall tread upon the tyrant's head,   45
Or wear it on my sword, yet my poor country
Shall have more vices than it had before,
More suffer, and more sundry ways than ever,
By him that shall succeed.
Macduff.   What should he be?
Malcolm.
It is myself I mean, in whom I know   50
All the particulars° of vice so grafted°
That, when they shall be opened,° black Macbeth
Will seem as pure as snow, and the poor state
Esteem him as a lamb, being compared
With my confineless harms.°
Macduff.   Not in the legions   55
Of horrid hell can come a devil more damned
In evils to top Macbeth.
Malcolm.   I grant him bloody,
Luxurious,° avaricious, false, deceitful,
Sudden,° malicious, smacking of every sin
That has a name: but there's no bottom, none,   60

---

41. **withal:** moreover.
42. **in my right:** on behalf of my claim.
43. **England:** the king of England.
44. **for:** despite.
51. **particulars:** special kinds. **grafted:** engrafted.
52. **opened:** in bloom (that is, revealed).
55. **confineless harms:** unbounded evils.
58. **Luxurious:** lecherous.
59. **Sudden:** violent.

In my voluptuousness:° your wives, your daughters,
Your matrons and your maids, could not fill up
The cistern of my lust, and my desire
All continent° impediments would o'erbear,
That did oppose my will. Better Macbeth   65
Than such an one to reign.
Macduff.   Boundless intemperance
In nature° is a tyranny; it hath been
Th' untimely emptying of the happy throne,
And fall of many kings. But fear not yet
To take upon you what is yours: you may   70
Convey° your pleasures in a spacious plenty,
And yet seem cold, the time° you may so hoodwink.
We have willing dames enough. There cannot be
That vulture in you, to devour so many
As will to greatness dedicate themselves,   75
Finding it so inclined.
Malcolm.   With this there grows
In my most ill-composed affection° such
A stanchless° avarice that, were I king,
I should cut off the nobles for their lands,
Desire his jewels and this other's house: 80
And my more-having would be as a sauce
To make me hunger more, that I should forge
Quarrels unjust against the good and loyal,
Destroying them for wealth.
Macduff.   This avarice
Sticks deeper, grows with more pernicious root   85
Than summer-seeming° lust, and it hath been

---

61. **voluptuousness:** lust.
64. **continent:** restraining.
67. **nature:** man's nature.
71. **Convey:** secretly manage.
72. **time:** here, people.
77. **ill-composed affection:** evilly compounded character.
78. **stanchless:** never-ending.
86. **summer-seeming:** youthful or transitory.

The sword of our slain kings.° Yet do not fear.
Scotland hath foisons to fill up your will
Of your mere own.° All these are portable,°
With other graces weighed.   90

Malcolm.
But I have none: the king-becoming graces,
As justice, verity, temp'rance, stableness,
Bounty, perseverance, mercy, lowliness,
Devotion, patience, courage, fortitude,
I have no relish of° them, but abound   95
In the division of each several crime,°
Acting it many ways. Nay, had I pow'r, I should
Pour the sweet milk of concord into hell,
Uproar° the universal peace, confound
All unity on earth.

Macduff.   O Scotland, Scotland!   100

Malcolm.
If such a one be fit to govern, speak:
I am as I have spoken.

Macduff.   Fit to govern!
No, not to live. O nation miserable!
With an untitled° tyrant bloody-sceptered,
When shalt thou see thy wholesome days again,   105
Since that the truest issue of thy throne
By his own interdiction° stands accursed,
And does blaspheme his breed?° Thy royal father
Was a most sainted king: the queen that bore thee,
Oft'ner upon her knees than on her feet,   110

---

87. **sword . . . kings:** the cause of death of our kings.
89. **foisons . . . own:** enough abundance of your own to satisfy your covetousness. **portable:** bearable.
95. **relish of:** taste for.
96. **division . . . crime:** variations of each kind of crime.
99. **Uproar:** put into a tumult.
104. **untitled:** having no right to the throne.
107. **interdiction:** curse; exclusion.
108. **breed:** ancestry.

Died° every day she lived. Fare thee well!
These evils thou repeat'st upon thyself
Hath banished me from Scotland. O my breast,
Thy hope ends here!

Malcolm.   Macduff, this noble passion,
Child of integrity, hath from my soul   115
Wiped the black scruples,° reconciled my thoughts
To thy good truth and honor. Devilish Macbeth
By many of these trains° hath sought to win me
Into his power; and modest wisdom° plucks me
From over-credulous haste: but God above   120
Deal between thee and me! For even now
I put myself to° thy direction, and
Unspeak mine own detraction;° here abjure
The taints and blames I laid upon myself,
For° strangers to my nature. I am yet   125
Unknown to woman, never was forsworn,
Scarcely have coveted what was mine own,
At no time broke my faith, would not betray
The devil to his fellow, and delight
No less in truth than life. My first false speaking   130
Was this upon myself. What I am truly,
Is thine and my poor country's to command:
Whither indeed, before thy here-approach,
Old Siward, with ten thousand warlike men,
Already at a point,° was setting forth.   135
Now we'll together, and the chance of goodness
Be like our warranted quarrel!° Why are you silent?

---

111. **Died:** that is, prepared for Heaven.
116. **scruples:** suspicions.
118. **trains:** plots.
119. **modest wisdom:** prudence.
122. **to:** under.
123. **detraction:** slander.
125. **For:** as.
135. **at a point:** prepared.
137. **the chance . . . quarrel:** May our chance of success equal the justice of
     our cause.

Macduff.

    Such welcome and unwelcome things at once
    'Tis hard to reconcile.

Enter a DOCTOR.

Malcolm.

    Well, more anon. Comes the king forth, I pray you?   140
Doctor.

    Ay, sir. There are a crew of wretched souls
    That stay° his cure: their malady convinces
    The great assay of art;° but at his touch,
    Such sanctity hath heaven given his hand,
    They presently amend.°
Malcolm.   I thank you, doctor.   145

                                Exit DOCTOR.

Macduff.

    What's the disease he means?
Malcolm.   'Tis called the evil:°

    A most miraculous work in this good king,
    Which often since my here-remain in England
    I have seen him do. How he solicits heaven,
    Himself best knows: but strangely visited° people,   150
    All swoll'n and ulcerous, pitiful to the eye,
    The mere° despair of surgery, he cures,
    Hanging a golden stamp° about their necks,
    Put on with holy prayers: and 'tis spoken,
    To the succeeding royalty he leaves   155
    The healing benediction. With this strange virtue°

---

142. **stay:** await.
143. **convinces . . . art:** defies the efforts of medical science.
145. **presently amend:** immediately recover.
146. **evil:** scrofula, called "the king's evil" because it allegedly could be
    cured by the king's touch.
150. **strangely visited:** oddly afflicted.
152. **mere:** utter.
153. **stamp:** coin.
156. **virtue:** power.

He hath a heavenly gift of prophecy,
And sundry blessings hang about his throne
That speak° him full of grace.

Enter ROSS.

Macduff.   See, who comes here?
Malcolm.
My countryman; but yet I know him not.   160
Macduff.
My ever gentle° cousin, welcome hither.
Malcolm.
I know him now: good God, betimes° remove
The means that makes us strangers!
Ross.   Sir, amen.
Macduff.
Stands Scotland where it did?
Ross.   Alas, poor country!
Almost afraid to know itself! It cannot   165
Be called our mother but our grave, where nothing°
But who knows nothing is once seen to smile;
Where sighs and groans, and shrieks that rent the air,
Are made, not marked;° where violent sorrow seems
A modern ecstasy.° The dead man's knell   170
Is there scarce asked for who, and good men's lives
Expire before the flowers in their caps,
Dying or ere they sicken.
Macduff.   O, relation
Too nice,° and yet too true!
Malcolm.   What's the newest grief?

---

159. **speak:** proclaim.
161. **gentle:** noble.
162. **betimes:** quickly.
166. **nothing:** no one.
169. **marked:** noticed.
170. **modern ecstasy:** ordinary emotion.
174. **relation / Too nice:** tale too accurate.

Ross.

    That of an hour's age doth hiss the speaker;°   175
    Each minute teems° a new one.

Macduff.   How does my wife?

Ross.

    Why, well.

Macduff.   And all my children?

Ross.   Well too.

Macduff.

    The tyrant has not battered at their peace?

Ross.

    No; they were well at peace when I did leave 'em.

Macduff.

    Be not a niggard of your speech: how goes't?   180

Ross.

    When I came hither to transport the tidings,
    Which I have heavily° borne, there ran a rumor
    Of many worthy fellows that were out;°
    Which was to my belief witnessed° the rather,
    For that I saw the tyrant's power° afoot.   185
    Now is the time of help. Your eye in Scotland
    Would create soldiers, make our women fight,
    To doff their dire distresses.

Malcolm.   Be't their comfort
    We are coming thither. Gracious England hath
    Lent us good Siward and ten thousand men;   190
    An older and a better soldier none
    That Christendom gives out.°

---

175. **That . . . speaker:** The report of the grief of an hour ago is hissed as
    stale news.
176. **teems:** gives birth to.
182. **heavily:** sadly.
183. **out:** up in arms.
184. **witnessed:** attested.
185. **power:** army.
192. **gives out:** reports.

Ross.   Would I could answer
    This comfort with the like! But I have words
    That would° be howled out in the desert air,
    Where hearing should not latch° them.
Macduff.   What concern they?   195
    The general cause or is it a fee-grief
    Due to some single breast?°
Ross.   No mind that's honest
    But in it shares some woe, though the main part
    Pertains to you alone.
Macduff.   If it be mine,
    Keep it not from me, quickly let me have it.   200
Ross.
    Let not your ears despise my tongue forever,
    Which shall possess them with the heaviest sound
    That ever yet they heard.
Macduff.   Humh! I guess at it.
Ross.
    Your castle is surprised;° your wife and babes
    Savagely slaughtered. To relate the manner,   205
    Were, on the quarry° of these murdered deer,
    To add the death of you.
Malcolm.   Merciful heaven!
    What, man! Ne'er pull your hat upon your brows;
    Give sorrow words. The grief that does not speak
    Whispers the o'er-fraught heart,° and bids it break.   210
Macduff.
    My children too?
Ross.   Wife, children, servants, all
    That could be found.

---

194. **would:** should.
195. **latch:** catch.
197. **fee-grief . . . breast:** that is, personal grief belonging to an individual.
204. **surprised:** suddenly attacked.
206. **quarry:** heap of slaughtered game.
210. **Whispers . . . heart:** whispers to the overburdened heart.

Macduff.   And I must be from thence!
  My wife killed too?
Ross.   I have said.
Malcolm.   Be comforted.
  Let's make us med'cines of our great revenge,
  To cure this deadly grief.   215
Macduff.
  He has no children. All my pretty ones?
  Did you say all? O hell-kite!° All?
  What, all my pretty chickens and their dam°
  At one fell swoop?
Malcolm.
  Dispute° it like a man.
Macduff.   I shall do so;   220
  But I must also feel it as a man.
  I cannot but remember such things were,
  That were most precious to me. Did heaven look on,
  And would not take their part? Sinful Macduff,
  They were all struck for thee! Naught° that I am,   225
  Not for their own demerits but for mine
  Fell slaughter on their souls. Heaven rest them now!
Malcolm.
  Be this the whetstone of your sword. Let grief
  Convert to anger; blunt not the heart, enrage it.
Macduff.
  O, I could play the woman with mine eyes,   230
  And braggart with my tongue! But, gentle heavens,
  Cut short all intermission;° front to front°
  Bring thou this fiend of Scotland and myself;
  Within my sword's length set him. If he 'scape,
  Heaven forgive him too!

---

217. **hell-kite:** hellish bird of prey.
218. **dam:** mother.
220. **Dispute:** counter.
225. **Naught:** wicked.
232. **intermission:** interval. **front to front:** forehead to forehead (that is, face to face).

Malcolm.   This time goes manly.   235
    Come, go we to the king. Our power is ready;
    Our lack is nothing but our leave.° Macbeth
    Is ripe for shaking, and the pow'rs above
    Put on their instruments.° Receive what cheer you
        may.
    The night is long that never finds the day.   [*Exeunt.*]   240

---

237. Our lack . . . leave: We need only to take our leave.
239. Put . . . instruments: arm themselves.

Act V

Scene 1. *Dunsinane. In the castle.*

Enter a DOCTOR *of physic and a waiting* GENTLEWOMAN.

Doctor. I have two nights watched with you, but can
    perceive no truth in your report. When was it she
    last walked?

Gentlewoman. Since his majesty went into the field, I
    have seen her rise from her bed, throw her nightgown   5
    upon her, unlock her closet,° take forth paper, fold it,
    write upon't, read it, afterwards seal it, and again
    return to bed; yet all this while in a most fast sleep.

Doctor. A great perturbation in nature, to receive at once
    the benefit of sleep and do the effects of watching!°   10
    In this slumb'ry agitation, besides her walking and
    other actual performances,° what, at any time, have
    you heard her say?

Gentlewoman. That, sir, which I will not report after her.

Doctor. You may to me, and 'tis most meet° you should.   15

Gentlewoman. Neither to you nor anyone, having no
    witness to confirm my speech.

Enter LADY MACBETH, *with a taper.*

    Lo you, here she comes! This is her very guise,° and,
    upon my life, fast asleep! Observe her; stand close.°

V.1.6. closet: chest.
  10. effects of watching: deeds of one who is awake.
  12. actual performances: deeds.
  15. meet: suitable.
  18. guise: custom.
  19. close: hidden.

Doctor. How came she by that light?   20

Gentlewoman. Why, it stood by her. She has light by
　　her continually. 'Tis her command.

Doctor. You see, her eyes are open.

Gentlewoman. Ay, but their sense° are shut.

Doctor. What is it she does now? Look, how she rubs   25
　　her hands.

Gentlewoman. It is an accustomed action with her, to
　　seem thus washing her hands: I have known her
　　continue in this a quarter of an hour.

Lady Macbeth. Yet here's a spot.   30

Doctor. Hark! she speaks. I will set down what comes
　　from her, to satisfy° my remembrance the more
　　strongly.

Lady Macbeth. Out, damned spot! Out, I say! One: two:
　　why, then 'tis time to do't. Hell is murky. Fie, my lord,   35
　　fie! A soldier, and afeard? What need we fear who
　　knows it, when none can call our pow'r to accompt?°
　　Yet who would have thought the old man to have had
　　so much blood in him?

Doctor. Do you mark that?   40

Lady Macbeth. The Thane of Fife had a wife. Where is
　　she now? What, will these hands ne'er be clean? No
　　more o' that, my lord, no more o' that! You mar all
　　with this starting.

Doctor. Go to,° go to! You have known what you should   45
　　not.

Gentlewoman. She has spoke what she should not, I am
　　sure of that. Heaven knows what she has known.

Lady Macbeth. Here's the smell of the blood still. All
　　the perfumes of Arabia will not sweeten this little   50
　　hand. Oh, oh, oh!

Doctor. What a sigh is there! The heart is sorely charged.°

24.　**sense:** powers of sight.
32.　**satisfy:** confirm.
37.　**to accompt:** into account.
45.　**Go to:** an exclamation.
52.　**charged:** burdened.

Gentlewoman. I would not have such a heart in my bosom for the dignity° of the whole body.

Doctor. Well, well, well—— 55

Gentlewoman. Pray God it be, sir.

Doctor. This disease is beyond my practice.° Yet I have known those which have walked in their sleep who have died holily in their beds.

Lady Macbeth. Wash your hands; put on your night- 60
gown; look not so pale! I tell you yet again, Banquo's buried. He cannot come out on's° grave.

Doctor. Even so?

Lady Macbeth. To bed, to bed! There's knocking at the gate. Come, come, come, come, give me your hand! 65
What's done cannot be undone. To bed, to bed, to bed!

Exit LADY MACBETH.

Doctor. Will she go now to bed?

Gentlewoman. Directly.

Doctor.
Foul whisp'rings are abroad. Unnatural deeds
Do breed unnatural troubles. Infected minds 70
To their deaf pillows will discharge their secrets.
More needs she the divine° than the physician.
God, God forgive us all! Look after her;
Remove from her the means of all annoyance,°
And still° keep eyes upon her. So good night. 75
My mind she has mated° and amazed my sight:
I think, but dare not speak.

Gentlewoman.   Good night, good doctor.

Exeunt.

---

54. **dignity:** worth; rank.
57. **practice:** professional skill.
62. **on's:** of his.
72. **divine:** priest.
74. **annoyance:** injury.
75. **still:** continuously.
76. **mated:** baffled.

Scene 2. *The country near Dunsinane.*

Drum and colors. Enter MENTEITH, CAITHNESS, ANGUS, LENNOX, SOLDIERS.

Menteith.
    The English pow'r° is near, led on by Malcolm,
    His uncle Siward and the good Macduff.
    Revenges burn in them; for their dear° causes
    Would to the bleeding and the grim alarm°
    Excite the mortified° man.
Angus.   Near Birnam Wood   5
    Shall we well meet them; that way are they coming.
Caithness.
    Who knows if Donalbain be with his brother?
Lennox.
    For certain, sir, he is not. I have a file°
    Of all the gentry: there is Siward's son,
    And many unrough° youths that even now   10
    Protest° their first of manhood.
Menteith.   What does the tyrant?
Caithness.
    Great Dunsinane he strongly fortifies.
    Some say he's mad; others, that lesser hate him,
    Do call it valiant fury: but, for certain,
    He cannot buckle his distempered° cause   15
    Within the belt of rule.°
Angus.   Now does he feel
    His secret murders sticking on his hands;

V.2.1. **pow'r:** army.
  3. **dear:** heartfelt.
  4. **alarm:** call to arms.
  5. **mortified:** half dead.
  8. **file:** list.
 10. **unrough:** beardless.
 11. **Protest:** assert.
 15. **distempered:** swollen with disease.
 16. **rule:** self-control.

Now minutely revolts upbraid° his faith-breach.
Those he commands move only in command,
Nothing in love. Now does he feel his title   20
Hang loose about him, like a giant's robe
Upon a dwarfish thief.

Mentieth.   Who then shall blame
His pestered° senses to recoil and start,
When all that is within him does condemn
Itself for being there?

Caithness.   Well, march we on,   25
To give obedience where 'tis truly owed.
Meet we the med'cine° of the sickly weal,°
And with him pour we, in our country's purge,
Each drop of us.°

Lennox.   Or so much as it needs
To dew° the sovereign° flower and drown the weeds.   30
Make we our march towards Birnam.

                              Exeunt, marching.

Scene 3. *Dunsinane. In the castle.*

Enter MACBETH, DOCTOR, *and* ATTENDANTS.

Macbeth.
Bring me no more reports; let them fly all!
Till Birnam Wood remove to Dunsinane
I cannot taint° with fear. What's the boy Malcolm?
Was he not born of woman? The spirits that know

---

18. **minutely revolts upbraid:** rebellions every minute rebuke.
23. **pestered:** tormented.
27. **med'cine:** that is, Malcolm. **weal:** commonwealth.
29. **Each . . . us:** that is, every last drop of our blood.
30. **dew:** bedew; water (and thus make grow). **sovereign:** royal; also, remedial.
V.3.3. **taint:** become infected.

All mortal consequences° have pronounced me thus: 5
"Fear not, Macbeth; no man that's born of woman
Shall e'er have power upon thee." Then fly, false thanes,
And mingle with the English epicures.
The mind I sway° by and the heart I bear
Shall never sag with doubt nor shake with fear.   10

Enter SERVANT.

The devil damn thee black, thou cream-faced loon!°
Where got'st thou that goose look?
Servant.
There is ten thousand——
Macbeth.   Geese, villain?
Servant.   Soldiers, sir.
Macbeth.
Go prick thy face and over-red° thy fear,
Thou lily-livered boy. What soldiers, patch?°   15
Death of° thy soul! Those linen° cheeks of thine
Are counselors to fear. What soldiers, whey-face?
Servant.
The English force, so please you.
Macbeth.
Take thy face hence.   [*Exit* SERVANT.]
                    Seyton!—I am sick at heart,
When I behold—Seyton, I say!—This push°   20
Will cheer me ever, or disseat° me now.
I have lived long enough. My way of life
Is fall'n into the sear,° the yellow leaf,

---

5. **mortal consequences:** future human events.
9. **sway:** move.
11. **loon:** fool.
14. **over-red:** cover with red.
15. **patch:** fool.
16. **of:** upon. **linen:** pale.
20. **push:** effort.
21. **disseat:** unthrone (with wordplay on *cheer,* pronounced "chair").
23. **sear:** withered.

And that which should accompany old age,
As honor, love, obedience, troops of friends,   25
I must not look to have; but, in their stead,
Curses not loud but deep, mouth-honor, breath,
Which the poor heart would fain deny, and dare not.
Seyton!

Enter SEYTON.

Seyton.
What's your gracious pleasure?
Macbeth.   What news more?   30
Seyton.
All is confirmed, my lord, which was reported.
Macbeth.
I'll fight, till from my bones my flesh be hacked.
Give me my armor.
Seyton.   'Tis not needed yet.
Macbeth.
I'll put it on.
Send out moe° horses, skirr° the country round.   35
Hang those that talk of fear. Give me mine armor.
How does your patient, doctor?
Doctor.   Not so sick, my lord,
As she is troubled with thick-coming fancies
That keep her from her rest.
Macbeth.   Cure her of that.
Canst thou not minister to a mind diseased,   40
Pluck from the memory a rooted sorrow,
Raze out° the written troubles of the brain,
And with some sweet oblivious° antidote
Cleanse the stuffed bosom of that perilous stuff
Which weighs upon the heart?
Doctor.   Therein the patient   45
Must minister to himself.

---

35. **moe:** more. **skirr:** scour.
42. **Raze out:** erase.
43. **oblivious:** causing forgetfulness.

Macbeth.

> Throw physic° to the dogs, I'll none of it.
> Come, put mine armor on. Give me my staff.
> Seyton, send out.—Doctor, the thanes fly from me.—
> Come, sir, dispatch.° If thou couldst, doctor, cast   50
> The water° of my land, find her disease
> And purge it to a sound and pristine health,
> I would applaud thee to the very echo,
> That should applaud again.—Pull't off, I say.—
> What rhubarb, senna, or what purgative drug,   55
> Would scour these English hence? Hear'st thou of
>   them?

Doctor.

> Ay, my good lord; your royal preparation
> Makes us hear something.

Macbeth.   Bring it° after me.

> I will not be afraid of death and bane°
> Till Birnam Forest come to Dunsinane.   60

Doctor (*aside*).

> Were I from Dunsinane away and clear,
> Profit again should hardly draw me here.   [*Exeunt.*]

Scene 4. *Country near Birnam Wood.*

Drum and colors. Enter MALCOLM, SIWARD, MACDUFF,
Siward's son YOUNG SIWARD, MENTEITH, CAITHNESS,
ANGUS, *and* SOLDIERS, *marching.*

Malcolm.

> Cousins, I hope the days are near at hand
> That chambers will be safe.°

Menteith.   We doubt it nothing.°

---

47. **physic:** medical science.
50. **dispatch:** hurry.
51. **cast / The water:** literally, analyze the urine.
58. **it:** the armor.
59. **bane:** destruction.
V.4.2. **That . . . safe:** that people will be safe in their bedrooms. **nothing:** not
at all.

Siward.

    What wood is this before us?

Menteith.   The Wood of Birnam.

Malcolm.

    Let every soldier hew him down a bough

    And bear't before him. Thereby shall we shadow   5

    The numbers of our host, and make discovery°

    Err in report of us.

Soldiers.   It shall be done.

Siward.

    We learn no other but° the confident tyrant

    Keeps still in Dunsinane, and will endure°

    Our setting down before't.

Malcolm.   'Tis his main hope,   10

    For where there is advantage to be given°

    Both more and less° have given him the revolt,

    And none serve with him but constrainèd things

    Whose hearts are absent too.

Macduff.   Let our just censures

    Attend the true event,° and put we on   15

    Industrious soldiership.

Siward.   The time approaches,

    That will with due decision make us know

    What we shall say we have and what we owe.°

    Thoughts speculative their unsure hopes relate,

    But certain issue strokes must arbitrate:°   20

    Towards which advance the war.° [*Exeunt, marching.*]

---

6. **discovery:** Macbeth's scouts.
8. **no other but:** nothing but that.
9. **endure:** allow.
11. **advantage . . . given:** afforded an opportunity.
12. **more and less:** high and low.
15. **just . . . event:** true judgments await the actual outcome.
18. **owe:** own. The contrast is between "what we shall say we have" and "what we shall really have."
20. **certain . . . arbitrate:** The definite outcome must be decided by battle.
21. **war:** army.

Scene 5. *Dunsinane. Within the castle.*

Enter MACBETH, SEYTON, *and* SOLDIERS, *with drum and colors.*

Macbeth.
Hang out our banners on the outward walls.
The cry is still "They come!" Our castle's strength
Will laugh a siege to scorn. Here let them lie
Till famine and the ague° eat them up.
Were they not forced° with those that should be ours,   5
We might have met them dareful,° beard to beard,
And beat them backward home.

A cry within of women.

                                    What is that noise?
Seyton.
It is the cry of women, my good lord.   [*Exit.*]
Macbeth.
I have almost forgot the taste of fears:
The time has been, my senses would have cooled   10
To hear a night-shriek, and my fell° of hair
Would at a dismal treatise° rouse and stir
As life were in't. I have supped full with horrors.
Direness, familiar to my slaughterous thoughts,
Cannot once start° me.

Enter SEYTON.

                                    Wherefore was that cry?   15
Seyton.
The queen, my lord, is dead.

V.5.4.   **ague:** fever.
    5.   **forced:** reinforced.
    6.   **met them dareful:** that is, met them boldly on the battlefield.
  11.   **fell:** pelt.
  12.   **treatise:** story.
  15.   **start:** startle.

Macbeth.
　　She should° have died hereafter;
　　There would have been a time for such a word.°
　　Tomorrow, and tomorrow, and tomorrow
　　Creeps in this petty pace from day to day,　　　　　　20
　　To the last syllable of recorded time;
　　And all our yesterdays have lighted fools
　　The way to dusty death. Out, out, brief candle!
　　Life's but a walking shadow, a poor player
　　That struts and frets his hour upon the stage　　　　25
　　And then is heard no more. It is a tale
　　Told by an idiot, full of sound and fury,
　　Signifying nothing.

Enter a MESSENGER.

　　Thou com'st to use thy tongue; thy story quickly!
Messenger.
　　Gracious my lord,　　　　　　　　　　　　　　　30
　　I should report that which I say I saw,
　　But know not how to do't.
Macbeth.　　　　　　　　　Well, say, sir.
Messenger.
　　As I did stand my watch upon the hill,
　　I looked toward Birnam, and anon, methought,
　　The wood began to move.
Macbeth.　　　　　　　　　Liar and slave!　　　35
Messenger.
　　Let me endure your wrath, if't be not so.
　　Within this three mile may you see it coming;
　　I say a moving grove.
Macbeth.　　　　　　　　If thou speak'st false,
　　Upon the next tree shalt thou hang alive,
　　Till famine cling° thee. If thy speech be sooth,°　　40

---

17. should: inevitably would.
18. word: message.
40. cling: wither. **sooth:** truth.

I care not if thou dost for me as much.
I pull in resolution,° and begin
To doubt° th' equivocation of the fiend
That lies like truth: "Fear not, till Birnam Wood
Do come to Dunsinane!" And now a wood   45
Comes toward Dunsinane. Arm, arm, and out!
If this which he avouches° does appear,
There is nor flying hence nor tarrying here.
I 'gin to be aweary of the sun,
And wish th' estate° o' th' world were now undone.   50
Ring the alarum bell! Blow wind, come wrack!
At least we'll die with harness° on our back. [*Exeunt.*]

Scene 6. *Dunsinane. Before the castle.*

Drum and colors. Enter MALCOLM, SIWARD, MACDUFF, *and their* ARMY, *with boughs.*

Malcolm.
Now near enough. Your leavy° screens throw down,
And show like those you are. You, worthy uncle,
Shall, with my cousin, your right noble son,
Lead our first battle.° Worthy Macduff and we°
Shall take upon's what else remains to do,   5
According to our order.°
Siward.   Fare you well.
Do we° but find the tyrant's power° tonight,
Let us be beaten, if we cannot fight.

---

42. **pull in resolution:** restrain confidence.
43. **doubt:** suspect.
47. **avouches:** asserts.
50. **estate:** orderly condition.
52. **harness:** armor.
V.6.1. **leavy:** leafy.
 4. **battle:** battalion. **we:** Malcolm uses the royal "we."
 6. **order:** plan.
 7. **Do we:** if we do. **power:** forces.

Macduff.

Make all our trumpets speak; give them all breath,
Those clamorous harbingers of blood and death.   10

Exeunt. Alarums continued.

Scene 7. *Another part of the field.*

Enter MACBETH.

Macbeth.

They have tied me to a stake; I cannot fly,
But bearlike I must fight the course.° What's he
That was not born of woman? Such a one
Am I to fear, or none.

Enter YOUNG SIWARD.

Young Siward.

What is thy name?

Macbeth.   Thou'lt be afraid to hear it.   5

Young Siward.

No; though thou call'st thyself a hotter name
Than any is in hell.

Macbeth.   My name's Macbeth.

Young Siward.

The devil himself could not pronounce a title
More hateful to mine ear.

Macbeth.   No, nor more fearful.

Young Siward.

Thou liest, abhorrèd tyrant; with my sword   10
I'll prove the lie thou speak'st.

Fight, and YOUNG SIWARD *slain.*

V.7.2. **course:** bout; round. (He has in mind an attack of dogs or men upon
a bear chained to a stake.)

Macbeth.   Thou wast born of woman.
But swords I smile at, weapons laugh to scorn,
Brandished by man that's of a woman born.   [*Exit.*]

Alarums. Enter MACDUFF.

Macduff.
That way the noise is. Tyrant, show thy face!
If thou be'st slain and with no stroke of mine,   15
My wife and children's ghosts will haunt me still.
I cannot strike at wretched kerns,° whose arms
Are hired to bear their staves.° Either thou, Macbeth,
Or else my sword, with an unbattered edge,
I sheathe again undeeded.° There thou shouldst be;   20
By this great clatter, one of greatest note
Seems bruited.° Let me find him, Fortune!
And more I beg not.   [*Exit. Alarums.*]

Enter MALCOLM *and* SIWARD.

Siward.
This way, my lord. The castle's gently rend'red:°
The tyrant's people on both sides do fight;   25
The noble thanes do bravely in the war;
The day almost itself professes° yours,
And little is to do.
Malcolm.   We have met with foes
That strike beside us.°
Siward.   Enter, sir, the castle.

                      Exeunt. Alarum.

---

17. **kerns:** foot soldiers (contemptuous).
18. **staves:** spears.
20. **undeeded:** that is, having done nothing.
22. **bruited:** reported.
24. **gently rend'red:** surrendered without a struggle.
27. **itself professes:** declares itself.
29. **That . . . us:** that is, who deliberately miss us as our comrades.

Scene 8. *Another part of the field.*

Enter MACBETH.

Macbeth.
Why should I play the Roman fool, and die
On mine own sword? Whiles I see lives,° the gashes
Do better upon them.

Enter MACDUFF.

Macduff. Turn, hell-hound, turn!
Macbeth.
Of all men else I have avoided thee.
But get thee back! My soul is too much charged°   5
With blood of thine already.
Macduff. I have no words:
My voice is in my sword, thou bloodier villain
Than terms can give thee out!°   [*Fight. Alarum.*]
Macbeth. Thou losest labor:
As easy mayst thou the intrenchant° air
With thy keen sword impress° as make me bleed: 10
Let fall thy blade on vulnerable crests;°
I bear a charmèd life, which must not yield
To one of woman born.
Macduff. Despair° thy charm,
And let the angel° whom thou still hast served
Tell thee, Macduff was from his mother's womb   15
Untimely ripped.

V.8.2. **Whiles . . . lives:** so long as I see living men.
   5. **charged:** burdened.
   8. **terms . . . out:** words can describe you.
   9. **intrenchant:** incapable of being cut.
  10. **impress:** make an impression on.
  11. **vulnerable crests:** heads that can be wounded.
  13. **Despair:** despair of.
  14. **angel:** that is, fallen angel; fiend.

Macbeth.

Accursèd be that tongue that tells me so,
For it hath cowed my better part of man!°
And be these juggling fiends no more believed,
That palter° with us in a double sense;   20
That keep the word of promise to our ear,
And break it to our hope. I'll not fight with thee.

Macduff.

Then yield thee, coward,
And live to be the show and gaze o' th' time:°
We'll have thee, as our rarer monsters° are,   25
Painted upon a pole,° and underwrit,
"Here may you see the tyrant."

Macbeth.   I will not yield,
To kiss the ground before young Malcolm's feet,
And to be baited° with the rabble's curse.
Though Birnam Wood be come to Dunsinane,   30
And thou opposed, being of no woman born,
Yet I will try the last. Before my body
I throw my warlike shield. Lay on, Macduff;
And damned be him that first cries "Hold, enough!"

Exeunt, fighting. Alarums.

Reenter fighting, and MACBETH *slain. Exit* MACDUFF, *with*
MACBETH. *Retreat and flourish.° Enter, with drum and
colors,* MALCOLM, SIWARD, ROSS, THANES, *and* SOLDIERS.

Malcolm.

I would the friends we miss were safe arrived.   35

---

18. **better . . . man:** manly spirit.
20. **palter:** equivocate.
24. **gaze . . . time:** spectacle of the age.
25. **monsters:** freaks.
26. **Painted . . . pole:** pictured on a banner set by a showman's booth.
29. **baited:** assailed (like a bear by dogs).
s.d. **Retreat and flourish:** trumpet call to withdraw, and fanfare.

Siward.

Some must go off;° and yet, by these I see,

So great a day as this is cheaply bought.

Malcolm.

Macduff is missing, and your noble son.

Ross.

Your son, my lord, has paid a soldier's debt:

He only lived but till he was a man;   40

The which no sooner had his prowess confirmed

In the unshrinking station° where he fought,

But like a man he died.

Siward.   Then he is dead?

Ross.

Ay, and brought off the field. Your cause of sorrow

Must not be measured by his worth, for then   45

It hath no end.

Siward.   Had he his hurts before?

Ross.

Ay, on the front.

Siward.   Why then, God's soldier be he!

Had I as many sons as I have hairs,

I would not wish them to a fairer death:

And so his knell is knolled.

Malcolm.   He's worth more sorrow,   50

And that I'll spend for him.

Siward.   He's worth no more:

They say he parted well and paid his score:°

And so God be with him! Here comes newer
     comfort.

Enter MACDUFF, *with Macbeth's head.*

---

36. **go off:** die (theatrical metaphor).

42. **unshrinking station:** that is, place at which he stood firmly.

52. **parted . . . score:** departed well and settled his account.

Macduff.

    Hail, king! for so thou art: behold, where stands
    Th' usurper's cursèd head. The time is free.°   55
    I see thee compassed° with thy kingdom's pearl,
    That speak my salutation in their minds,
    Whose voices I desire aloud with mine:
    Hail, King of Scotland!

All.   Hail, King of Scotland!

Flourish.

Malcolm.

    We shall not spend a large expense of time   60
    Before we reckon with your several loves,°
    And make us even with you. My thanes and kinsmen,
    Henceforth be earls, the first that ever Scotland
    In such an honor named. What's more to do,
    Which would be planted newly with the time°—   65
    As calling home our exiled friends abroad
    That fled the snares of watchful tyranny,
    Producing forth the cruel ministers°
    Of this dead butcher and his fiendlike queen,
    Who, as 'tis thought, by self and violent hands°   70
    Took off her life—this, and what needful else
    That calls upon us,° by the grace of Grace
    We will perform in measure, time, and place:°
    So thanks to all at once and to each one,
    Whom we invite to see us crowned at Scone.   75

                              Flourish. Exeunt omnes.

---

55. **The time is free:** The world is liberated.
56. **compassed:** surrounded.
61. **reckon . . . loves:** reward the devotion of each of you.
65. **What's . . . time:** What else must be done that should be newly established in this age.
68. **ministers:** agents.
70. **self . . . hands:** her own violent hands.
72. **calls upon us:** demands my attention.
73. **in . . . place:** fittingly, at the appropriate time and place.

Macbeth's Porter

In Act II, Scene 3, Macbeth's porter appears and banters with Macduff. Why does the porter—speaking a gross, drunken rigmarole—appear just at this point in the play, right after the murder of Duncan? Is this not a monstrous interruption?

One way to account for the scene is to remind ourselves that Shakespeare was writer-in-residence to a company of actors and was therefore bound to provide parts for every member in every play—even a part for the chief comedian in a tragedy. But this is not a satisfactory explanation, because it was not characteristic of Shakespeare merely to do what was expected of him as a professional writer; he always did something more, almost making a virtue out of theatrical necessity. And so, as a second explanation of the porter's scene, some critics have argued that it is designed to provide comic relief from the tense aftermath of Duncan's murder. But this also is not a convincing reason, because the scene actually increases tension rather than relieving it. As Macbeth and his wife stand whispering about the evil thing they have done, they—and the audience—are startled to hear a loud and totally unexpected knocking on the main gate of the castle. Even a hardened criminal would be startled by the coincidence of these events, and Macbeth and his wife are mere beginners in crime. While they hastily retreat into their bedroom, the porter (the word means "door tender") shuffles onstage to answer the knocking at his leisure, thus prolonging the interval between the murder and its discovery and greatly increasing suspense. And after all, suspense is what makes drama interesting.

Theatergoers in Shakespeare's day were accustomed to comic porters; they were familiar figures in miracle plays, in which they kept the gates of Hell. They were expected to be droll and at the same time sinister. "Who's there, i' th' name of Beelzebub?" asks Macbeth's porter, referring to one of the chief devils and implying that the castle is a place the Devil occupies. And indeed it already has become Hell, which is as much a state of mind as a particular place. Lady Macbeth has called for the "smoke of hell" in Act I, and Macbeth has been unable to say "Amen" when Duncan's men cried "God bless us!" in Act II. To cut out the porter's scene, as many directors (and many editors of school texts) have done, is to weaken the fabric of the play.

The King's Evil

In Act IV, Scene 3, Malcolm and Macduff, exiled from Scotland, discuss the characteristics of a good king and praise King Edward, who has given them political asylum in England. Edward, a saintly monarch known to history as "the Confessor," was believed to have the gift of healing any of his subjects who suffered from scrofula, or tuberculosis of the lymphatic glands. This ailment, which was primarily a disease of children, was known as the king's evil. Long before Shakespeare's time, the custom of being touched by the king was abandoned, but King James revived the practice and his successors continued it for a century or so. The eighteenth-century writer Samuel Johnson, who was scrofulous as a child, was one of the last English people to receive the royal touch.

The conversation between Malcolm and Macduff not only indirectly compliments King James but also implicitly condemns Macbeth, a kingly killer rather than a healer of children. Edward cures evil; Macbeth *is* evil.

Hecate: Queen of the Night

Hecate (here pronounced in two syllables, with the accent on the first: hek'it) is a figure from Greek mythology, a queen of the night and protector of witches and enchanters. This character comes from books, unlike the witches, who were based on older, usually widowed women, whose solitary lives placed them at the margins of Scottish society. Every theatergoer would find the witches believable, and every educated person would know that King James had written an important treatise called *Daemonologie,* asserting that witches "are channels through which the malignity of evil spirits might be visited upon human beings."

Most Shakespearean scholars believe that the scenes involving Hecate (Act III, Scene 5; Act IV, Scene 1) were written by somebody other than Shakespeare and introduced into *Macbeth* at some time before 1623, when the play was first printed. This other writer has never been positively identified, although some people think it was Thomas Middleton (d. 1627), a contemporary of Shakespeare and a fellow writer for the King's Men. Two songs, the first beginning with the words "Come away" (Act III, Scene 5) and the second with "Black Spirits" (Act IV, Scene 1), were also added to the Hecate scenes, and these songs are indeed by Middleton, the complete texts of them occurring in his thriller *The Witch.*

And so the practice of adding things to *Macbeth* began very early, and it has continued throughout most of the play's long stage history. The supernatural elements seem to invite directors to devise spectacles and take liberties, especially with the witches, who have been flown on wires in some productions and whose parts have been played by ballet dancers in others.

Soliloquies and Asides

Renaissance playwrights had two useful devices for revealing to an audience or reader a dramatic character's innermost thoughts and feelings: soliloquies and asides.

A **soliloquy** is a meditative speech in which a character, usually alone onstage and pretending that the audience is not present, thinks out loud. Everybody understands that the speaker of a soliloquy tells the truth freely and openly, however discreditable that truth may be. For instance, in his famous soliloquy beginning "To be or not to be," Shakespeare's Hamlet admits to the audience that he is thinking of committing suicide.

Asides are much shorter than soliloquies but just as truthful. **Asides** are a character's private comments on what is happening at a given moment in a play. They are spoken out of the side of the mouth, so to speak, for the benefit of the audience; the other characters onstage pretend that they do not hear them. For example, Macbeth's asides in Act I, Scene 3, tell us that he cannot put the witches' prophecies out of his mind.

Macbeth's tragic decline can best be traced in his solo speeches—his asides and soliloquies. The most important of these, which are what make the play so interesting psychologically, occur as follows:

Act I, Scene 3, lines 130–142
Act I, Scene 4, lines 48–53
Act I, Scene 7, lines 1–28
Act II, Scene 1, lines 33–64
Act III, Scene 1, lines 48–72
Act IV, Scene 1, lines 144–156
Act V, Scene 3, lines 19–29
Act V, Scene 5, lines 9–15

Early in the play the soliloquies show Macbeth's indecision and his fierce inner conflict; then, after he succumbs to evil, they show the terror in his soul and his inability to recover his lost innocence. At times they even show that he is reconciled to his murderous career, especially after the second set of prophecies gives him a false sense of security. But finally the soliloquies show his despair and loss of feeling about, and interest in, life itself. All of these changing states of mind are expressed in powerful images that help the audience share Macbeth's suffering. In contrast, we see Lady Macbeth mainly from the outside, though an attentive reader can find speeches in which she also reveals feelings. In *Macbeth* the inner, spiritual catastrophe parallels the outer, physical catastrophe.

The Mystery of Evil

*M*acbeth fascinates us because it shows, perhaps more clearly than any of Shakespeare's other tragedies, how a character can change as a result of what he does. *Macbeth* also shows that crime does not pay, but that smug cliché is not very relevant to the play: Macbeth is "caught" as soon as he understands the witches' prophecy, and his mental anguish begins before he commits any crimes.

At the start of the play, the mere thought of committing a murder terrifies Macbeth, although he is no novice at carving up men in battle. But it is one thing to fight openly, quite another to kill stealthily. His wife says her great warrior husband Macbeth is "too full o' th' milk of human kindness." Shakespeare apparently wants us to think of Macbeth as a good man and to feel sympathetic toward him even after he becomes a murderer. When Duncan's body is found, Macbeth does not feel excited about becoming king; instead, he mutters to himself, "The wine of life is drawn." He can't enjoy his kingly state; he is too terrified by what he is doing. "Full of scorpions is my mind," he says to his wife. He lives in such constant terror that by the end of the play he is numb to all feeling—even to the death of his beloved wife. A "dead butcher," Malcolm calls him: an automatic killer.

Lady Macbeth's deterioration is different from her husband's but just as dramatic. Legally, she is only an accomplice, never an actual murderer. But she is the first to decide that Duncan must die; Macbeth wavers right up to the last moment. After the first murders, she exerts immense control over herself while he surrenders to his nerves. But she does eventually crack under the strain. Malcolm might not have called her a "fiendlike queen" after her death had he known how much she suffered from pangs of conscience. Both Macbeth and his wife are moral beings who excite our pity rather than our contempt or disgust.

But why do they commit their crimes? The customary answer to this question—that they are ambitious—leads only to another question: Why are they so ambitious that they are willing to commit such crimes? Ultimately, these questions are unanswerable, because evil is as mysterious as it is real. Shakespeare makes no attempt to solve the mystery; instead, in *Macbeth*, he uses language to make it even more mysterious.

The world of *Macbeth* is filled, from beginning to end, with mysterious and repulsive images of evil.

The Imagery: Darkness, Night, Blood

First of all, there are the witches. The play opens with the three witches performing their sinister rites and chanting, "Fair is foul, and foul is fair," blurring the differences between these opposites. Macbeth's first speech joins the same opposites, as though they were synonyms: "So foul and fair a day I have not seen." Macbeth's speech thus establishes a connection between himself and the witches even before he meets them.

Shakespeare's audience would have immediately recognized the witches as embodiments of evil in league with Satan himself. Several times they refer to themselves as the "weird sisters"— *weird* here meaning maliciously and perversely supernatural, possessing harmful powers given them by evil spirits in the form of nasty pets such as old gray tomcats and toads. English and Scottish witches are not like the Fates of Greek mythology, whose baleful influence could not be resisted. Rather, they are tempters of a kind that Shakespeare's contemporaries believed they should always avoid. One of the witches seems to foretell Macbeth's future by saying, "All hail, Macbeth, that shalt be king hereafter!" After an inner struggle, and under the influence of his wife's goading, Macbeth chooses to make "hereafter" happen immediately. Nowhere in the play do the witches *cause* Macbeth to make this wicked decision. Rather, he voluntarily surrenders himself, following a visionary dagger—a manifestation of his decision—that leads him into Duncan's bedroom. Having once given in to evil, Macbeth is thereafter under the control of evil forces stronger than his own moral sense.

Shakespeare expresses these evil forces in images of darkness, night, and blood. He has Banquo call the weird sisters "instruments of darkness," linking them to the thick gloom that pervades the whole play and provides a cover under which evil can do its work. Even in daylight, Macbeth and his wife invoke the night: "Come, thick night," Lady Macbeth cries as part of her prayer asking evil spirits to "unsex" her. Macbeth also calls for night to come, to blindfold "the tender eye of pitiful day" so that the killers he has hired can safely murder innocent Banquo and his son.

By setting many of the violent scenes at night and by making the scenes in *Macbeth* "murky," full of "fog and filthy air," and pierced by the cries of owls, Shakespeare suppresses all the pleasant associations night might have, especially as the time for refreshing sleep. Just as he commits his first murder, Macbeth thinks he hears a horrible voice crying "Macbeth does murder sleep"; thereafter, he becomes an insomniac and his wife a sleepwalker. Darkness, voices, ghosts, hallucinations—these are used to express Macbeth's and his wife's surrender to evil and their subsequent despair.

Evil in *Macbeth* takes the form of violence and bloodshed. Right after the opening scene with the witches, a man covered with gashes appears before King Duncan, who asks, "What bloody man is that?" Between this scene and the final one, in which Macbeth's bleeding and "cursèd" head is displayed on a pike, human blood hardly stops running. Images of blood appeal not only to our sense of sight but also to our sense of touch (Macbeth's bloody and secret murders are "sticking on his hands" in the last act), and even to our sense of smell ("Here's the smell of the blood still," Lady Macbeth moans in Act V as she holds out her "little hand"). Such imagery is designed to make us feel moral revulsion, not just physical disgust: Bloodshed leads only to more bloodshed.

The Poetry: Evoking the Dark Night

All this imagery reminds us that *Macbeth* is a poem as well as a play—a dramatic poem sharing many of the characteristics of lyric poetry. The most obvious of these is **meter,** here the unrhymed iambic pentameter, or **blank verse,** that Shakespeare's predecessor Christopher Marlowe established as the appropriate medium for tragedy. Poetry is to tragedy as singing is to opera: It elevates and enhances the emotional impact of the experience being communicated. Indeed, without the poetry there could be no tragedy, because without it Shakespeare could not have evoked the dark night into which Macbeth's soul sinks. And a tragic poet is much more concerned with states of mind and feeling than with physical action. Macbeth shares with Shakespeare's other great tragic heroes—Hamlet, Lear, Othello—the ability to express in eloquent, moving language whatever he is feeling. One of the most famous speeches of this kind occurs when, near the end of his bloody career, Macbeth sums up what life means to him:

> Out, out, brief candle!
> Life's but a walking shadow, a poor player
> That struts and frets his hour upon the stage
> And then is heard no more. It is a tale
> Told by an idiot, full of sound and fury,
> Signifying nothing.
> —Act V, Scene 5, lines 23–28

The bitter nihilism of these metaphors suggests that Macbeth is already dead in spirit, although his body must undergo a last battle. By murdering Duncan, he has murdered more than sleep: He has destroyed himself.

An Essay

from On the Knocking at the Gate in *Macbeth*
by Thomas De Quincey

Thomas De Quincey (1785–1859) was an English essayist and critic.

From my boyish days I had always felt a great perplexity on one point in *Macbeth*. It was this: The knocking at the gate which succeeds to the murder of Duncan produced to my feelings an effect for which I never could account. The effect was that it reflected back upon the murderer a peculiar awfulness and a depth of solemnity; yet, however obstinately I endeavored with my understanding to comprehend this, for many years I never could see *why* it should produce such an effect.

. . . At length I solved it to my own satisfaction; and my solution is this: —Murder, in ordinary cases, where the sympathy is wholly directed to the case of the murdered person, is an incident of coarse and vulgar horror; and for this reason—that it flings the interest exclusively upon the natural but ignoble instinct by which we cleave to life: an instinct which, as being indispensable to the primal law of self-preservation, is the same in kind (though different in degree) amongst all living creatures. This instinct, therefore, because it annihilates all distinctions, and degrades the greatest of men to the level of "the poor beetle that we tread on," exhibits human nature in its most abject and humiliating attitude. Such an attitude would little suit the purposes of the poet. What then must he do? He must throw the interest on the murderer. Our sympathy must be with *him* (of course I mean a sympathy of comprehension, a sympathy by which we enter into his feelings, and are made to understand them—not a sympathy of pity or approbation). In the murdered person, all strife of thought, all flux and reflux of passion and of purpose, are crushed by one overwhelming panic; the fear of instant death smites him "with its petrific mace."[1] But in the murderer, such a murderer as a poet will condescend to, there must be raging some great storm of passion—jealousy, ambition, vengeance, hatred—which will create a hell within him; and into this hell we are to look.

In *Macbeth,* for the sake of gratifying his own enormous and teeming faculty of creation, Shakespeare has introduced two murderers: and, as usual in his hands, they are remarkably discriminated: but—though in Macbeth the strife of mind is greater than in his wife, the tiger spirit not so awake, and his feelings caught chiefly by contagion from her—yet, as both were finally involved in the guilt of murder, the murderous mind of necessity is finally to be presumed in both. This was to be expressed; and, on its own account, as well as to make it a more proportionable antagonist to the unoffending nature of their victim, "the gracious Duncan," and adequately to expound "the deep damnation of his taking off," this was to be expressed with peculiar energy. We were to be made to feel that the human nature—i.e., the divine nature of love and mercy, spread through the hearts of all creatures, and seldom utterly withdrawn from man—was gone, vanished, extinct, and that the fiendish nature had taken its place. And, as this effect is marvelously accomplished in the *dialogues* and *soliloquies* themselves, so it is finally consummated by the expedient under consideration; and it is to this that I now solicit the

---

1. petrific mace: stone club. This is an allusion to Milton's *Paradise Lost* (Book X, line 294), in which Death wields a "mace petrific."

reader's attention. If the reader has ever witnessed a wife, daughter, or sister in a fainting fit, he may chance to have observed that the most affecting moment in such a spectacle is *that* in which a sigh and a stirring announce the recommencement of suspended life.

. . . All action in any direction is best expounded, measured, and made apprehensible, by reaction. Now, applying this to the case in *Macbeth:* Here, as I have said, the retiring of the human heart and the entrance of the fiendish heart was to be expressed and made sensible. Another world has stepped in; and the murderers are taken out of the region of human things, human purposes, human desires. They are transfigured: Lady Macbeth is "unsexed"; Macbeth has forgot that he was born of woman; both are conformed to the image of devils; and the world of devils is suddenly revealed. But how shall this be conveyed and made palpable? In order that a new world may step in, this world must for a time disappear. The murderers and the murder must be insulated—cut off by an immeasurable gulf from the ordinary tide and succession of human affairs—locked up and sequestered in some deep recess; we must be made sensible that the world of ordinary life is suddenly arrested, laid asleep, tranced, racked into a dread armistice; time must be annihilated, relation to things without abolished; and all must pass self-withdrawn into a deep syncope[2] and suspension of earthly passion. Hence it is that, when the deed is done, when the work of darkness is perfect, then the world of darkness passes away like a pageantry in the clouds: The knocking at the gate is heard, and it makes known audibly that the reaction has commenced; the human has made its reflux upon the fiendish; the pulses of life are beginning to beat again; and the reestablishment of the goings-on of the world in which we live first makes us profoundly sensible of the awful parenthesis that had suspended them.

2. **syncope** (sin′kə·pē): unconsciousness.

The Bard and the Database

In literary circles it's known as the Authorship Question: Was William Shakespeare, the actor from Stratford-on-Avon, actually the author of the greatest poetry the world has ever known?

This question has been around since the 1700s, and over the years people have proposed as many as fifty-eight various writers as possible authors of Shakespeare's plays and poems, ranging from Sir Francis Bacon to Sir Walter Raleigh to Queen Elizabeth I herself.

Matching Shakespeare. Hoping to apply some twentieth-century computer technology to this seventeenth-century problem, Professor Ward Elliott of Claremont McKenna College near Los Angeles created a database of Renaissance literature, including the King James Bible, all of Shakespeare's poetry, and material from twenty-seven of the most promising candidates, and embarked upon his "Matching Shakespeare" study. Elliott's plan was first to identify Shakespeare's unique style through computer analysis and then to compare this with the styles of various writers to see if any matched up.

Elliott's "Matching Shakespeare" study applied dozens of different linguistic tests, but five conventional tests and a powerful new one proved most accurate. The conventional tests measured features like the number of relative clauses and hyphenated compound words and the length of words and sentences, and the new test used a pattern recognition technique.

And the real Shakespeare is. What have the tests shown? Did Shakespeare write Shakespeare? On the basis of his studies,

Elliott believes that he has been able to eliminate all the principal candidates. Every writer failed at least one of the conventional tests, with some failing four or five. On the other hand, Shakespeare's writings all fell within a consistent profile. Although the study does not prove that it was Shakespeare himself who wrote the works attributed to him, Elliott (along with most reputable scholars) feels that it does demonstrate that one individual *did* write them all.

Why has such a fuss been made about the authorship of Shakespeare's works? In part, it's because people cannot believe that someone who led such a seemingly ordinary life could have been such a genius. Shakespeare still confounds all the scholarly detectives who continue to debate the "Authorship Question."

A Parody

Macbeth and the Witches
by Richard Armour

Nothing is impervious to parody, not even the high seriousness of a play like Shakespeare's Macbeth. *In the following piece, from* Twisted Tales from Shakespeare, *Richard Armour presents another view of the three weird sisters. You and your classmates might want to write a parody of your own.*

Three witches, extremely weird sisters, are having a picnic amidst thunder and lightning somewhere in Scotland. Judging from their appearance, they were placed one-two-three in the Edinburgh Ugly Contest.

"When shall we three meet again in thunder, lightning, or in rain?" asks one of them. They hate nice weather and are happiest when they are soaking wet and their hair is all stringy.

"When the hurly-burly's[1] done, when the battle's lost and won," another replies. A battle is going on between the forces of Duncan, the King of Scotland, and some Norwegians, assisted by the rebel Thane of Cawdor. At the moment it's looking good for Duncan, because two of his generals, Macbeth and Banquo, have cunningly put bagpipes into the hands of the enemy, who are blowing their brains out.

---

1. See also hurdy-gurdy, hunky-dory, and okey-dokey.

The witches hear some dear friend[2] calling and depart. "Fair is foul, and foul is fair," they comment philosophically as they leave. This must have been pretty upsetting to any moralists, semanticists, or baseball umpires who chanced to overhear them.

Shortly afterward, the battle having been won by Macbeth and the weather having turned bad enough to be pleasant, the witches meet again.

"Where hast thou been, Sister?" asks one.

"Killing swine," the second replies. All three of them have been busy doing similar diverting things, and one of them happily shows the others the thumb of a drowned sailor which she is adding to her thumb collection.[3]

Macbeth and Banquo come by at this point, on their way to inform the King that they have defeated the rebels. They would rather tell him in person than render a report in triplicate.

"Speak, if you can," says Macbeth boldly to the hags. "What are you?" He rather thinks they are witches but would like to hear it from their own skinny lips.

The witches start hailing.[4] They hail Macbeth as Thane of Glamis and Thane of Cawdor and say he will be King Hereafter. Not to leave Banquo out, they hail him as "lesser than Macbeth, and greater." (The witches are masters of gobbledyspook.) He won't be a king, they say, but he'll beget kings, and now they have to begetting along.

Macbeth knows he is Thane of Glamis, but has no idea (or didn't have until now) of becoming Thane of Cawdor or King Hereafter. "Stay, you imperfect speakers, tell me more," he commands. But the witches, perhaps not liking the way he refers to their elocution, vanish into thin air, making it slightly thicker.

---

2. A cat and a toad. Witches have to make friendships where they can.
3. In a comedy, this would be considered tragic relief.
4. Until now it has been raining.

While Macbeth is meditating about what the witches have forecast for him, a couple of the King's henchmen, straight from a busy day of henching, ride up. They bring word that Duncan is liquidating the Thane of Cawdor and giving his title to Macbeth, it being an inexpensive gift. (Duncan, as King of Scotland, was Scotcher than anybody.)

"Look how our partner's rapt," remarks Banquo, noticing that Macbeth, stunned with all the good news, acts as if he has been struck on the noggin. But Macbeth is only lost in thought and will find his way out presently. Thus far the witches have been batting 1,000, and Macbeth is beginning to take more than a casual interest in Duncan's health.[5]

5. Henceforth, when he says "How are you?" to the King, it will be a bona fide question.

[These are Richard Armour's footnotes.]

World Literature

Canto 34
from The Inferno of Dante
by Dante Alighieri
translated by Robert Pinsky

If you had to name the three most evil people of all time, who would be on your list? The great medieval Italian writer Dante Alighieri (1265–1321) wrote an epic poem called The Divine Comedy, *in which he imagined a journey through Hell, Purgatory, and Paradise. At the very pit of Hell, Dante put Judas Iscariot. Dante imagined Judas to be the most evil man in the world because he betrayed Jesus Christ to the Romans. The other two sinners whom Dante puts in the very jaws of Satan may come as a surprise—although you have probably met them in Shakespeare: Brutus and Cassius, the conspirators of ancient Rome who plotted the assassination of Julius Caesar. Another surprise is Dante's description of the worst part of Hell: Instead of a burning pit of fire and brimstone, the bottom of Dante's Hell is a ghastly, windswept lake of ice.*

Dante's journey to Hell takes place in the first part of The Divine Comedy. *(The epic is a comedy in the sense that it has a happy ending.) Led by the poet Virgil, who to Dante symbolizes reason, Dante travels to the Inferno down a deep funnel that bores into the center of the*

earth. Around this abysmal cavity run nine ledges, or circles, which grow ever narrower as the cavity bores deeper
into the earth. In each circle a certain kind of sin is punished. The sins of the flesh are in the upper circle, where
punishment is mildest. Sins of anger are punished in the
middle, and sins against reason are punished in the low-
est circles, where torment is greatest.

From the Inferno, Dante and his guide ascend gradually through Purgatory. Then Virgil turns his companion
over to a woman named Beatrice ("blessed"), who leads
Dante into Paradise; there he is granted a blissful vision
of God and salvation. What Dante learns of sin from
visiting the agonies of Hell, of renunciation from witness-
ing the trials of Purgatory, and of joy from sharing the
glories of Paradise will turn him from error forever.

As this part of The Inferno opens, Dante and his guide
approach the innermost circle of Hell. It is dominated by
the gigantic winged figure of Satan, frozen in ice.

"And now, *Vexilla regis prodeunt*
    Inferni°—therefore, look," my master said
    As we continued on the long descent,

"And see if you can make him out, ahead."
    As though, in the exhalation of heavy mist   5
    Or while night darkened our hemisphere, one spied

A mill—blades turning in the wind, half-lost
    Off in the distance—some structure of that kind
    I seemed to make out now. But at a gust

---

2. ***Vexilla regis prodeunt / Inferni:*** Latin for "The banners of the king of
   Hell advance." These words perversely echo a well-known Latin hymn.

Of wind, there being no other shelter at hand,   10
  I drew behind my leader's back again.
  By now (and putting it in verse I find

Fear in myself still) I had journeyed down
  To where the shades were covered wholly by ice,°
  Showing like straw in glass—some lying prone,   15

And some erect, some with the head toward us,
  And others with the bottoms of the feet;
  Another like a bow, bent feet to face.

When we had traveled forward to the spot
  From which it pleased my master to have me see   20
  That creature° whose beauty once had been so great,

He made me stop, and moved from in front of me.
  "Look: here is Dis," he said, "and here is the place
  Where you must arm yourself with the quality

Of fortitude." How chilled and faint I was   25
  On hearing that, you must not ask me, reader—
  I do not write it; words would not suffice:

I neither died, nor kept alive—consider
  With your own wits what I, alike denuded
  Of death and life, became as I heard my leader.   30

---

14. where . . . ice: This is Judecca (jōō·dek'ə), the final division of Cocytus
   (kō·sīt'əs) and the innermost part of Hell. Judecca is named for Judas
   Iscariot, who betrayed Jesus.
21. creature: Satan. Dante also calls him by the names Lucifer, Beelzebub,
   and Dis. Before Satan rebelled against God and was cast down from
   Heaven, he was an angel of tremendous beauty.

The emperor of the realm of grief protruded
    From midbreast up above the surrounding ice.
    A giant's height, and mine, would have provided

Closer comparison than would the size
    Of his arm and a giant. Envision the whole   35
    That is proportionate to parts like these.

If he was truly once as beautiful
    As he is ugly now, and raised his brows
    Against his Maker—then all sorrow may well

Come out of him. How great a marvel it was   40
    For me to see three faces° on his head:
    In front there was a red one; joined to this,

Each over the midpoint of a shoulder, he had
    Two others—all three joining at the crown.
    That on the right appeared to be a shade   45

Of whitish yellow; the third had such a mien
    As those who come from where the Nile descends.
    Two wings spread forth from under each face's chin,

Strong, and befitting such a bird, immense—
    I have never seen at sea so broad a sail—   50
    Unfeathered, batlike, and issuing three winds

That went forth as he beat them, to freeze the whole
    Realm of Cocytus that surrounded him.
    He wept with all six eyes, and the tears fell

---

41. three faces: grotesque perversion of the Trinity.

Over his three chins mingled with bloody foam.   55
    The teeth of each mouth held a sinner, kept
    As by a flax rake: thus he held three of them

In agony. For the one the front mouth gripped,
    The teeth were as nothing to the claws, which sliced
    And tore the skin until his back was stripped.   60

"That soul," my master said, "who suffers most,
    Is Judas Iscariot; head locked inside,
    He flails his legs. Of the other two, who twist

With their heads down, the black mouth holds the shade
    Of Brutus: writhing, but not a word will he scream;   65
    Cassius is the sinewy one on the other side.

But night is rising again, and it is time
    That we depart, for we have seen the whole."
    As he requested, I put my arms round him,

And waiting until the wings were opened full   70
    He took advantage of the time and place
    And grasped the shaggy flank, and gripping still,

From tuft to tuft descended through the mass
    Of matted hair and crusts of ice. And then,
    When we had reached the pivot of the thighs,°   75

Just where the haunch is at its thickest, with strain
    And effort my master brought around his head
    To where he'd had his legs: and from there on

---

75. pivot of the thighs: This midpoint of Satan's body is also the center of
    the earth. At this spot, Virgil turns himself upside down because
    henceforth the travelers must journey *up* Satan's legs in order to reach
    the surface of the Southern Hemisphere.

He grappled the hair as someone climbing would—
    So I supposed we were heading back to Hell.   80
    "Cling tight, for it is stairs like these," he sighed

Like one who is exhausted, "which we must scale
    To part from so much evil." Then he came up
    Through a split stone, and placed me on its sill,

And climbed up toward me with his cautious step.   85
    I raised my eyes, expecting I would see
    Lucifer as I left him—and saw his shape

Inverted, with his legs held upward. May they
    Who are too dull to see what point I had passed
    Judge whether it perplexed me. "Come—the way   90

Is long, the road remaining to be crossed
    Is hard: rise to your feet," the master said,
    "The sun is at mid-tierce."° We had come to rest

In nothing like a palace hall; instead
    A kind of natural dungeon enveloped us,   95
    With barely any light, the floor ill made.

"Before I free myself from the abyss,
    My master," I said when I was on my feet,
    "Speak, and dispel my error: where is the ice?

And how can he be fixed head-down like that?   100
    And in so short a time, how can it be
    Possible for the sun to make its transit

93. mid-tierce: Formerly, tierce was the period from 6:00 to 9:00 A.M. (the first third of the day), so mid-tierce is about 7:30 A.M. In Hell, the sun is never consulted in telling time, but now that Dante and Virgil have emerged from Hell, they use the sun for that purpose.

From evening to morning?" He answered me,
   "You imagine you are still on the other side,
   Across the center of the earth, where I   105

Grappled the hair on the evil serpent's hide
   Who pierces the world. And all through my descent,
   You were on that side; when I turned my head

And legs about, you passed the central point
   To which is drawn, from every side, all weight.   110
   Now you are on the opposite continent

Beneath the opposite hemisphere to that
   Which canopies the great dry land therein:
   Under the zenith of that one is the site

Whereon the Man was slain° who without sin   115
   Was born and lived; your feet this minute press
   Upon a little sphere whose rounded skin

Forms the Judecca's other, outward face.
   Here it is morning when it is evening there;
   The one whose hair was like a ladder for us   120

Is still positioned as he was before.
   On this side he fell down from Heaven; the earth,
   Which till then stood out here, impelled by fear

---

115. Under the zenith . . . slain: Under the zenith, or highest point, of the
Northern Hemisphere's sky—a point reached directly through the earth
and thus "opposite" where Dante and Virgil now stand—is the city of
Jerusalem, the site where Jesus Christ, "the Man," was slain.

Veiled itself in the sea and issued forth
    In our own hemisphere. And possibly,   125
    What now appears on this side° fled its berth

And rushing upward left a cavity:
    This hollow where we stand." There is below,
    As far from Beelzebub as one can be

Within his tomb, a place one cannot know   130
    By sight, but by the sound a little runnel°
    Makes as it wends the hollow rock its flow

Has worn, descending through its winding channel:
    To get back up to the shining world from there
    My guide and I went into that hidden tunnel;   135

And following its path, we took no care
    To rest, but climbed: he first, then I—so far,
    Through a round aperture I saw appear

Some of the beautiful things that Heaven bears,
When we came forth, and once more saw the stars.°   140

---

126. **What now appears on this side:** The island of Mount Purgatory, the
    pinnacle at which a sinner makes a total renunciation of sin, was
    apparently formed out of the inner earth displaced by Lucifer's fall.
    Climbing this peak will be the next leg of Dante's journey.
131. **runnel:** stream. This rivulet may derive from the river Lethe, the river of
    forgetfulness in classical mythology.
140. **stars:** As he does in the *Purgatorio* and *Paradiso,* Dante ends the *Inferno*
    with the word *stars.* For him stars are symbols of hope toward which the
    soul constantly moves. The time—just before dawn on Easter morning—
    is also symbolic of hope.

Shakespeare's Language
by John Algeo

John Algeo is a professor of English at the University of Georgia at Athens. He is coauthor, with Thomas Pyles, of The Origins and Development of the English Language.

Shakespeare's language is an early form of Modern English, basically the same kind of English we speak. But we need glosses, or explanations, for some words and phrases because English has changed during the past four hundred years.

Speaking the Speech: Shakespeare's Pronunciation

The actors who pronounced Shakespeare's lines on the stage of the Globe Theater would not have sounded like modern actors, American or British. We need not be concerned with the details of their pronunciation, but some differences are obvious even from the written text of the plays. For example, Shakespeare's contemporaries, like English speakers today, used a great many contractions. But they contracted words differently from the way we do.

Shakespeare liked to contract the pronouns that begin with vowels (*us* and *it*), as the following examples show:

. . . we / Shall take upon's what else remains to do . . .

. . . To mend it, or be rid on't [of it].

. . . for't must be done to-night.

What is't that moves your Highness?

Shakespeare also frequently omitted unstressed syllables from the middle of words (as we still do in words like *fam'ly*):

. . . o'er the rest . . .

. . . will these hands ne'er be clean?

. . . my near'st [nearest] of life . . .

Thou marvel'st at my words . . .

A whole syllable could be omitted from the beginning of a word if it was unstressed (as in the shortening of *because* to *'cause*, a change we still make today):

. . . 'cause he fail'd . . .

Point against point, rebellious arm 'gainst arm . . .

. . . 'Twixt this and supper.

. . . if he 'scape . . .

I 'gin to be aweary of the sun . . .

Some of Shakespeare's words are stressed on different syllables from those we would now accent. For example, in "Stop up th' access and passage to remorse," the iambic rhythm of the line shows us that Shakespeare pronounced *access* "acCESS," rather than "ACcess," as we would.

Other words have changed their forms in various ways since Shakespeare's day. In *Macbeth*, we find *murther* for *murder*, *afeard* for *afraid*, *aweary* for *weary*, and *alarum* for *alarm*.

Shakespeare's Grammar

Although Shakespeare's grammar is essentially the same as ours, it differs in numerous minor ways.

Shakespeare could use *which* where we use *who* to refer to a person: ". . . the slave / Which ne'er shook hands." He could also use *the which*, especially with broad or unstated antecedents: "He only liv'd but till he was a man; / The which [his manhood] no sooner had his prowess confirm'd, . . . / But like a man he died."

Shakespeare could also use the pronoun *who* in an indefinite sense, for which we use *the one who:* "Who was the thane, lives yet."

In present-day English, we use *mine* as a pronoun and *my* to modify a noun: "It's mine" but "It's my book." Shakespeare used both forms to modify nouns: *mine* before words beginning with a vowel, and *my* before words beginning with a consonant, just as we use *an* and *a* today ("an orange," "a lemon"): "Ha! they pluck out mine eyes. / Will all great Neptune's ocean wash this blood / Clean from my hand?"

Today we generally use only a single pronoun for the person or people we talk to: *you* (with its possessives *your* and *yours*). Shakespeare had a choice between *th-* forms (*thou, thee, thy, thine*) and *y-* forms (*ye, you, your, yours*). *Thou* and *ye* were subject forms, like *I; thee* and *you* were object forms, like *me.*

Th- forms were used in talking to one person with whom the speaker was intimate (wife, husband, bosom buddy) or to whom the speaker was socially superior (child, servant, subject). *Y-* forms were used in talking to several people, or to one person who was a social equal but not an intimate friend or who was a superior (parent, boss, king). In the singular, *th-* forms showed intimacy or superiority; *y-* forms showed equality or servility.

Shakespeare made careful use of the different connotations of *th-* and *y-* forms. When Macbeth and Banquo meet the weird sisters (Act I, Scene 3), they address the witches with *y-* forms because the two soldiers are in awe of these supernatural women; the witches, however, use *th-* forms for Macbeth and Banquo, thereby asserting their superiority over the mere mortals.

Macbeth and Banquo normally address one another with *y-* forms because, though equals, they are not intimates. At the beginning of Act III, however, when Banquo is thinking about the foul deeds that Macbeth has obviously used to come to the throne, he uses *th-* forms for Macbeth, since he regards

Macbeth's murderous actions as having made a moral inferior of him. Banquo can think what he wants, but when Macbeth actually appears, Banquo addresses him with *y*- forms again. For Banquo to have called King Macbeth *thou* to his face would have been an insulting breach of etiquette.

The verb in Shakespeare's day had a special ending, *-st*, to go with *thou* as a subject, thus: "thou know'st," "thou didst," and "thou hast." It also had an alternative ending, *-th*, for the third-person singular ending, *-s*, that we still use today. Shakespeare could use "he knows" or "he knoweth," "he does" or "he doth," and "he has" or "he hath." The two forms meant the same thing, although the *-s* ending was more common, and the *-th* ending probably sounded rather formal or old-fashioned even in Shakespeare's day. Sometimes Shakespeare used the two together—"The earth hath bubbles, as the water has"—with no apparent difference in meaning.

Shakespeare could omit the helping verb *do* in questions and negative sentences where we must have it:

Live you? [Do you live?]
Ride you this afternoon? [Do you ride this afternoon?]
Fail not our feast. [Don't fail (to be at) our feast.]
He loves us not. [He doesn't love us.]

On the other hand, Shakespeare could use an unstressed *do* where we cannot:

. . . swimmers, that do cling together . . .
. . . such things here as we do speak about . . .
His wonders and his praises do contend . . .
. . . the earth / Was feverous, and did shake.

Shakespeare had a wider choice of past participles than we do in standard English today, although some of Shakespeare's forms have survived even today in nonstandard speech:

I have spoke. [for *spoken*]

And his great love . . . hath holp him. [for *has helped*]

Shakespeare could use forms of *be* instead of *have* to form the perfect tense of verbs indicating motion: "They are not yet come back."

Where we would say "Come on, let's go to the king," Shakespeare has simply "Come, go we to the King." Shakespeare's *go we* is an old first-person command that is more direct than the *let's go* form we now prefer.

In both Shakespeare's English and ours, noun phrases may consist of a determiner (like *the, a, my*), an adjective, and a noun: *the old house.* However, in short expressions used to address a person, Shakespeare could put the adjective first: "Gentle my Lord" (for "My gentle Lord") and "Gracious my Lord" (for "My gracious Lord").

Some of what we consider mistakes today are also found in Shakespeare. They are actually old ways of using English that have fallen out of favor in standard English; for example:

There's daggers in men's smiles . . . [There are daggers]

Who I myself struck down . . . [Whom I myself struck down]

. . . ask'd for who . . . [for whom]

Shakespeare's Words

In some respects, Shakespeare's vocabulary was more complex than ours. We commonly use three words for location: *here, there,* and *where.* Shakespeare had nine, because in addition to those three, six others were available that are now rare, if not archaic: *hence, thence, whence* ("from here," "from there," "from where") and *hither, thither, whither* ("to here," "to there," "to where"):

Whence cam'st thou, worthy Thane? [Where did you come from?]

I will thither. [I will go (to) there.]
Whither should I fly? [Where should I fly to?]

Shakespeare uses other words that are now rare or obsolete:

I say sooth . . . [I tell the truth] [We still have *sooth* in the word *soothsayer* ("truth teller").]
This diamond he greets your wife withal [with] . . .
Send out moe [more] horses. [In Early Modern English, *moe* referred to number, *more* to size.]

In Shakespeare's plays some of the words that strike us as fancy were fancy even when he used them. They were "inkhorn terms"—words borrowed from the classical languages and used for their mouth-filling and impressive sounds, as well as for their subtleties of meaning. Just after he has stabbed King Duncan, Macbeth says that his hand will never be clean again, but will rather

The multitudinous seas incarnadine . . .

He means that the blood on his hands would make "the many seas red," but the word *multitudinous* seems to mean far more than the short word *many,* and the literal meaning of *incarnadine* ("to turn into the blood-red color of raw flesh") is especially appropriate to Macbeth's actions and state of mind. Shakespeare was using fancy words—but for a purpose.

The trickiest words in Shakespeare, however, are those that look familiar but whose meanings are different from those of their present-day versions. They are false friends that make us think we understand what the language means while in fact indicating something different from what we expect. Here are a few examples:

Sweno, the Norways' king, craves composition [agreement; peace terms]. . . .

Are ye fantastical [illusory; imaginary], or that indeed /
Which outwardly ye show [seem; appear]?

Say from whence / You owe [own; have] this strange intelligence [information].

Sleep, that knits up [straightens out] the raveled sleave
[tangled thread] of care. . . . [The image of reknitting the
sleeve of a sweater that has unraveled makes sense but is
wrong.]

Because of differences like these between Shakespeare's
English and ours, it takes some effort for us to read his plays
and poetry. What we can get from the reading, however, is
well worth the effort.